CENACOLO
by Joseph Orbi

RedCrest Tower, Ltd.

2010

ISBN: 978-0-9661619-7-7

Printed in the United States of America

*For information regarding production
rights and/or royalties, please call
213.533.0774, 787.439.9011 or write to
info@redcresttower.com*

RedCrest Tower, Ltd
51 Calle Ruiz Belvis,
San Juan, PR 00917

Characters

In Order of Appearance

i

Time & Setting

1498
Some times in Milan
Some times in Rome

ii

FIRST ACT

Scene i

Downstage Right, *an* **Old Man**, *dressed in a monk's habit, with long white hair and beard, sits on a wooden box, in his narrow cell. He writes furiously under the dim light of a single candle stub. After a moment, he lays down his quill, contemplates the wide manuscript, slowly and with great difficulty, gets on his feet and limps forward, holding the book to his bosom.*

OLD MAN: It has taken me fifty years to compile this manuscript.

He extends the book to show the **Audience**, *then caresses the cover with his fingers.*

OLD MAN: I am an old man now; shrunken, withered away. There is no semblance of what I once was. My tired eyes, that under a set of these perfectly white and extravagant, shaggy eyebrows are half-shut most of the time, are failing rapidly, an indication of that inevitable day when they will fail altogether, forever, to be awakened once again only by the brilliant splendor of the afterlife. But my mind, that inspired and divine repository of experience, is still able to reach back, back, into a distant past. It is then I remember how handsome I was and the love for life and the ambition that I once cradled in my bosom. *(pause)* Everything was different then. Love and war were pursued with equal relish and morality never made it past the portals of the church. Truth is the passing of time distorts history, much like an old, warped and faded looking-glass that has been locked away in a dusty room will lose its talent for reflection. Even chronicled events will be misunderstood when culture, habits and mannerisms are misinterpreted and that which seems obvious in the present may have been something else altogether. To confuse matters further, Mankind's own insecure eccentricities tend to view anything it does not understand as enlightened, attributing brilliance to gibberish and mysticism to fiddle-faddle. How else do you explain calling that fellow Vasari, an historian? What does he know? He–he was not there! I was! This–Vasari–Vasari was a fool! *(Long pause)* It was in 1498. Italy was still haunted by the Middle Ages–

Lights go down on the **Old Man** *as* **Upstage**, *a shop appears. It has a rustic sign that reads:* "**Tomassino-Sweets**". *Enter* **Salai**. *He carries a note in one hand. Pause. He reads the note. He frowns, takes a deep sigh and goes in the shop.*

TOMASSINO: Salai! My goodness, where have you been?
SALAI: Busy.
TOMASSINO: Too busy to visit your old friend?
SALAI: Too busy and too poor.
TOMASSINO: Too poor, eh? *(Laughs)* I know how you feel, my boy. I am poor too. Or do you think I like being holed up in this room mixing, cooking and baking all day, sweating like a pig and smelling like a peasant? *(pause)* Or should I say smelling like a pig and sweating like a peasant? Where you heading?
SALAI: *(Shows the note)* Next door—to Lucca's.

The boy looks at the colorful bags of candy on the wall.

TOMASSINO: How much do you have, eh? Your master is a rich man. He should give you an allowance every now and then.
SALAI: He says I—we should pay him.
TOMASSINO: Why not? He is a great master.
SALAI: And we are his slaves!
TOMASSINO: Are you, now? *(Playfully shoves* **Salai***)* So, come work for me. Mind you, I would not pay you either but at least you could eat candy all day. You can help me make deliveries and I'll teach you everything there is to know about making candy. That way, when I'm old and don't want to work anymore, you can take over the shop. *(Pause)* What do you say? You want to be my apprentice?
SALAI: It's all right. I'll get by.
TOMASSINO: *(Laughs)* Yes, I have no doubt you will. Tell you what—How about doing me a favor?

Brings out a fancy box of candy.

TOMASSINO: Ten soldi worth of comfits, my friend—all yours if you deliver this to the citadel. *(Pause)* This box is brought here every other day, for me to fill it up with Princess Beatrice's favorite

TOMASSINO: *(Cont.)* –comfits, the same kind you like so much except with a hazel nut inside. Most times a soldier picks up the box but it seems the army is on maneuvers and they forgot to pick up the candy. That means two things: Princess Beatrice will not get her candy and Tomassino will not get paid. I can't leave the shop–mother's been very sick lately–

SALAI: I'll do it!

TOMASSINO: I had a feeling you would.

Tomassino *tosses a bag of candy to the boy.*

TOMASSINO: Catch! *(Pause)* I wished all my clients loved candy as much as you. I'd be as rich as Messer Lucca. He makes more money than anyone. Maybe I should sell artist's supplies. What do you think?

SALAI: Don't. Pigment tastes like shit.

TOMASSINO: Your master–will be angry?

SALAI: For my master to be angry my master has to know what I'm doing. Since we're not going to tell him– *(pops a comfit in his mouth)* –I don't think he'll be angry at all.

TOMASSINO: You better be going.

SALAI: Now? But–Messer Lucca?

TOMASSINO: He won't be in for some time. He and his wife–she's a crone, you know–they got into a drunken fight last night and she won–cracked his head with a broom. Leave the note with me. I'll make sure he gets it–sometime today.

Salai *gives the note to* **Tomassino**.

TOMASSINO: *(Reads)* Lucca: I am sending you my servant, Salai– *(To* **Salai***)* "Servant?"

Salai *shrugs.*

SALAI: You won't forget?

TOMASSINO: I won't forget. Trust me.

The boy pops a piece of candy in his mouth and picks up the box of candy from the counter.

SALAI: To the palace!

Exit **Salai**. **Tomassino** *Calls out.*

TOMASSINO: Tell the guard Tomassino sent you!

Scene ii

Same time. The refectory at Santa Maria Delle Grazie . **Upstage Center**, *a large scaffold approximately ten feet off the ground and set in front of a large tarp, which is held up by ropes and covers the entire wall of the dining room. SOUND: The choir of friars in the background.*

LORENZO: I need blue.
ANTONIO: I don't have any.
LORENZO: Who's mixing?
MARCO: Salai.
ANTONIO: Salai?
LORENZO: Great!
ANTONIO: He's not here.
LORENZO: *(Sarcastic)* Really?
MARCO: Maestro sent him for—
LORENZO: Oh, shut up!
MARCO: I won't and I won't mix, either!

Enter **Fra Bandello**.

BANDELLO: Where has he run off to now? *(Pause)* You there— where is he?
LORENZO: Who?
BANDELLO: Your master.
LORENZO: I don't know.
MARCO: He's been gone since—
BANDELLO: He's with the horse, right?
MARCO: I can't say. I don't know where he is.
BANDELLO: *(Aside)* How can he possibly ever hope to finish? I'll be dead a hundred years before he's done. It is impossible! *(Aside)* He spends the time running in and out of the dining room all day! And when he is not running in and out, he is wasting endless hours with arms folded, standing before the picture; pondering and wondering; cerebrating and inspecting, thinking everything over, weighing the possibilities against each other, revolving and resolving the whole process in his head, changing the same, only

BANDELLO: *(Cont.)* –to dwell on the changes, propose alternatives, envision further chaos, debate it at length, consider it anon, put his arms to his side, forget what he was supposed to do in the first place, notice the day is making way for night, take off his apron, go home and end up doing nothing! *(Pause)* Once, when the glare of the sun was at its height and the streets in Milan deserted from the heat, Maestro Leonardo rushed from the citadel—where he's working on the blasted horse—and without seeking shade and by the shortest way, returned to the refectory, took a thin brush, dipped it in paint, added a touch, dropped the brush, ran down the scaffold and disappeared for three days. *(Pause)* And these—hooligans! Who ever imagined he would turn our refectory into a Greek gymnasium! Oh, when, when, will it stop?

Enter **Leonardo.**

LEONARDO: Goooood morning—so good of you to drop by, brother!

BANDELLO: *(Startled)* I should say that to you, Maestro. It is indeed good to see you for once! Where were you yesterday and the day before? *(Points to the boys)* They were here. But their master had something better to do, I guess. The abbot asked me just now, less than ten minutes ago, 'how is the wall doing?' says he. 'It is not,' says I! *(Pause)* Well, I don't care so much about the abbot. He's as guilty as you are, Maestro and I will not let him shirk his responsibility. It was he, after all, who thought it would be a good idea to have you work on this—on this wall. I, on the other hand—

LEONARDO: You are right, brother. You are always right. Now, why don't you be right again and leave so we can continue to waste our time decorating your monastery? *(Calls)* Marco! *(To* **Bandello***)* You see, my dear, most of my work is accomplished before I set paint to canvas—or to a wall, for that matter. It is the way I formulate concepts out of which I create a masterpiece!

Marco *pulls on the rope and the tarp falls to reveal the 13 feet 10 inches by 29 feet 7½ inches fresco the* <u>Cenacolo</u>.

The fresco is luminous, its colors bright and with its perspective extraordinarily clear. The painting is almost complete, except for the face of Jesus Christ and that of Judas Iscariot. Pause.

BANDELLO: It's the same as three months back.

LEONARDO: Think so?

BANDELLO: Maestro, do you have any idea the protestations I have to listen to every day? Every morning, as I prepare for mass, I am assailed by my brothers. They don't say good morning, or wonder if it will rain at last. No. They gather by my door and hurl questions at me, as if I was the one keeping them out of this room. They want to know, they have a right to know and so do I. When? When is the great Leonardo Da Vinci going to finish painting that wall? When is the horrible noise, the disgusting, nauseating smell of turpentine, the unsightly plaster everywhere and the unbecoming conduct of your—apprentices—stop? In other words, when will your invasion end? Someone else would have finished long ago!

LEONARDO: Ah but the point is, brother, someone else is not me. Antonio, don't dawdle, make yourself useful—clean the brushes. Lorenzo, put together some whites and blues for the windows. *(To **Bandello**)* And you—don't stand there like a stick of wax, use your influence with the Almighty and get me Jesus Christ.

BANDELLO: I beg your pardon?

LEONARDO: I'll tell you why it is taking so long. I have been looking for the Christ and the Judas for one and a half years. Where can I find someone with the loving virtue required to model for the Christ. And where can I find a man so insidious that he alone can stand for Judas? Come, come, brother, you are supposed to know more about these things than I do.

BANDELLO: Well— *(Pause)* A new man arrived last night from Ticino, you may want to see him.

LEONARDO: What for?

BANDELLO: He might catch your fancy.

LEONARDO: Why would I want anyone to catch—my fancy?

BANDELLO: I meant, perhaps he is what you are looking for.

LEONARDO: For what?

BANDELLO: For the wall.

LEONARDO: *(Pause)* For the Judas?

BANDELLO: For the Christ!

LEONARDO: Are you sure? I have known friars that could have found reasonable employment impersonating the Judas—anytime.

BANDELLO: Would you like to see him or not?

LEONARDO: *(Pause)* Yes, I guess. *(Pause)* What can I lose but more time! What's his name?

BANDELLO: Marcelino. *(Pause)* I almost forgot—a man was looking for you. *(Pause)* Two men, really, because he was accompanied by a friar—*not* one of us. *(Pause)* I told him—them—to come here—that you were apt to turn up—*sometime*. They must have gotten tired of waiting. God knows I am. Please—keep this door shut! The noise and the smell of—

LEONARDO: Did he give his name, brother?

BANDELLO: No!

Exit **Bandello**.

LEONARDO: Strange name.

LORENZO: Who?

LEONARDO: Marcelino.

ANTONIO: Why?

LEONARDO: For a friar—most of them are named after one saint or another.

MARCO: Paul!

LORENZO: Joseph!

ANTONIO: Peter!

LORENZO: Marcelino!

LEONARDO: No, it doesn't sound right.

Blackout.

Scene iii

Same time. The citadel; **Bernardino's** *study .* **Bernardino** *stands by his table, facing* **Salai**.

BERNARDINO: Candy for the princess?
LUDOVICO: *(Off)* Bernardino!
BERNARDINO: And—what is your name, my lovely?
SALAI: Giacomo Andrea, if it please you, sir.
BERNARDINO: How old are you, pretty Giacomino?
SALAI: Fourteen, sir.

Bernardino *takes one of the pieces of candy and gives it to the boy.*

BERNARDINO: *(Pause)* Eat it.
SALAI: But—but they're for her ladyship!
BERNARDINO: *(Smiles)* Yes, we know. However, we must make sure the candy is not poisoned.
SALAI: Poisoned? Oh, no, sir!

Salai *eats the candy.*

BERNARDINO: So—you run errands for Tomassino?
SALAI: No, sir. I—
LUDOVICO: *(Off)* Bernardino!
BERNARDINO: Never mind, my lovely Giacomo. We will have to talk some other time. *(Gives him a few coins)* For your troubles, Giacomo.
SALAI: *(Bows)* Thank you, sir!
LUDOVICO: *(Off)* Bernardino!!!

Bernardino *pats the boy on the cheek.*

BERNARDINO: The guard will show you outside.

Blackout.

Scene iv

Same time. The refectory . Enter **Machiavelli** *and* **Fra Valentino**.

MACHIAVELLI: Maestro Leonardo!

LEONARDO: Who is there? Step in, I cannot see you.

MACHIAVELLI: A man is prudent not to reveal himself until assured he's welcome.

LEONARDO: Machiavelli!

MACHIAVELLI: Ah—recognized the voice?

LEONARDO: Recognized the wit! *(Pause)* Dear me, what a wonderful surprise! What—it must be five, six years at least?

MACHIAVELLI: At least.

LEONARDO: How did you find me?

MACHIAVELLI: I asked the prior, who said you were not around so, I asked a beggar.

LEONARDO: A beggar?

MACHIAVELLI: That is to say I could have asked anyone where you were. You are as well known as the Duke.

LEONARDO: Indeed.

MACHIAVELLI: Maestro Leonardo Da Vinci, this is Fra Valentino. *(Pause)* I'm sorry to barge in on you like this. I should have written I was coming to see you. I know how busy you are.

LEONARDO: Busy for others, not my friends.

MACHIAVELLI: You are too kind. *(Pause)* Look, any chance you can get away for a few hours?

LEONARDO: *(Pause)* I'd never hear the end of it from Fra Bandello. *(To* **Fra Valentino***)* He's the prior—you met him already, I think? *(Points at the wall)* They say I'm taking too long on—

MACHIAVELLI: And how long is that?

LEONARDO: Going on three years. *(Pause)* I have a better idea. What I mean is—why don't you and—

MACHIAVELLI: Fra Valentino.

LEONARDO: Yes—why not come to supper, tonight?

MACHIAVELLI: Have you taught the boys to cook?

LEONARDO: Everything but! *(Pause)* I do have a woman who is a real artist with the sauce.

MACHIAVELLI: Yes—I would like that. *(Pause)* I'm curious to see how the great Leonardo Da Vinci is doing these days—if what I've heard is true.

LEONARDO: You will be disappointed. *(Pause)* Any suggestions, brother?

FRA VALENTINO: Impressive.

LEONARDO: *(Laughs)* Shall we say seven o'clock?

MACHIAVELLI: Seven.

LEONARDO: I'll send for you. Where are you staying?

MACHIAVELLI: We are not. We are leaving this very night. And don't worry, I know where you live.

Machiavelli *smiles, tilts his head in obeisance and opens the back door.*

Enter **Salai**. *He collides with* **Machiavelli** *and* **Fra Valentino**.

SALAI: Oh, beg your pardon, Master!

LEONARDO: Salai!

MACHIAVELLI: *(To* **Leonardo***)* These lads—they are quite animated.

LEONARDO: If animated means reckless and ill-mannered!

MACHIAVELLI: Goodbye, Maestro.

Exit **Machiavelli** *and* **Fra Valentino**.

LEONARDO: I told you a thousand times, this is not the coliseum! You're here to work, not to run or knock people about!

SALAI: Yes, Maestro, I am sorry.

ANTONIO: What a clumsy whoreson, you are.

SALAI: Vaffanculo!

LEONARDO: *(Angry)* Salai!

SALAI: Sorry, Maestro.

LEONARDO: You have wasted enough time, already! Come— diligence, diligence! Get to it!

ANTONIO: Yes, Maestro!

MARCO: I am the only one who does anything around here.

LEONARDO: Not enough! *(Pause)* Where was I? *(Pause)* Blues and whites; silver and gold.

LEONARDO: *(Cont.)* Sunlight from the rear, the green pasture can use more splendor. The windows need greater definition. *(Pause)* If only I knew where to find you, my Lord Savior. If only I knew where to find you, Judas Iscariot. *(Pause)* What a delightful paradox; a lovely dream, a foul nightmare; a soft autumn night, a suffocating summer noon; sparkling water running down a mountain brook, a rotting sewer; a brilliant incandescent light and the void of the dark; Christ and the betrayer.

Blackout.

Scene v

Same time. The citadel; **Ludovico's** *study . A small statue of a horse is displayed on a pedestal.*

Enter **Bernardino**.

BERNARDINO: Good morning, Excellency!

LUDOVICO: It was about time! Where have you been? I've been calling you for hours!

BERNARDINO: I must be losing my hearing, sire. I only heard my name bounce off the walls of the citadel three times. Of course, as soon as I heard your call, I ran all the way here, even leaped over a rose bush that—well, it seems to have kept a piece of my hose.

LUDOVICO: Where is my wife?

BERNARDINO: She is in the garden counting butterflies.

LUDOVICO: Counting butter—? Why?

BERNARDINO: It is my guess, Excellency, that Princess Beatrice is so young and—innocent, her interests have not broadened for greater measure and whims—such as wanting to know how many butterflies inhabit the gardens around the citadel—encroach her youthful and tender intellect.

LUDOVICO: Pointless, I am sure.

BERNARDINO: Ah, that might be true, Excellency, indeed but being pointless is the prerogative of the Princess, just like spending a fortune on a giant horse is the prerogative of the Moor.

LUDOVICO: Are you telling me I cannot afford the horse?

BERNARDINO: No, Excellency, I would never say that. I am simply stating the obvious—the horse is a very expensive horse. Maestro Leonardo is asking—no, forgive me, I am sorry, Maestro Leonardo never asks for anything—Maestro Leonardo demands so much bronze for the horse that I do not know what to do. It is such a staggering amount of metal, that either you import it at great cost, or melt half the cannons protecting the duchy which will cost you even more.

LUDOVICO: We must find a way.

BERNARDINO: Why don't you levy an equestrian tax on every citizen that owns more than one horse—for the horse?

LUDOVICO: *(Laughs)* Oh, that is funny, Counselor. Any more taxes and they will run both of us out of town. No, no taxes. Think of something. You of all people know how important that horse is for me. It has to be magnificent.

BERNARDINO: It costs too much.

LUDOVICO: What if I say the cost does not matter?

BERNARDINO: *(Bows)* You can say what you please, Your Excellency.

LUDOVICO: *(Points at the horse)* You forget that it is my father who will be sitting on top of the horse.

BERNARDINO: I know, I understand and I agree. The monument should be built—has to be built, Your Excellency. And I know, I understand and I wholeheartedly concur that the monument must be extraordinary. However, why does it have to be so eeenooormous?

LUDOVICO: It is meant to impress.

BERNARDINO: By what it represents, not by its size. Excellency, if I may be perfectly candid. This—Maestro Leonardo has a most peculiar habit. He inflates, expands, amplifies, broadens and extends everything out of proportion, dimension and symmetry. This—artist lacks what I like to call, a sense of practicality. For instance, when you asked him to paint a fresco in the refectory of the monastery, he made up his mind to paint, not a section of the wall, as anyone with an ounce of common sense might have but the whole side of the building. The same thing happened when you engaged him to do the monument to your illustrious father. By the time Maestro Leonardo is finished, that monument will be bigger, larger, taller, wider and more expensive than any other monument, memorial, obelisk, mausoleum, shrine or statue in the world with the possible exception of the Sphinx, the pyramids of Egypt and the Colossus of Rhodes.

LUDOVICO: You're not mincing words today, Counselor. Are you displeased with Maestro Leonardo?

BERNARDINO: Displeased? I? No, not displeased. As my dear late wife used to say, to know what it is to be displeased one needs to know what it is to be pleased and I am yet to find anything pleasing about Maestro Leonardo.

LUDOVICO: You're being unfair.

BERNARDINO: Perhaps. I lack your good nature and charity, which tends to see the best in people, Excellency.

BERNARDINO: *(Cont.)* I have always said that you are too forbearing. Let us just say I find Maestro Leonardo a presumptuous fop who masks his shortcomings with arrogance.

LUDOVICO: *(Chuckles)* I shudder to think what he thinks of you.

BERNARDINO: I know that Maestro Leonardo resents it when I demand an accounting of his expenses and I have been told—many times—that he feels it is an affront that he should ask me for an appointment to meet with Your Excellency. Yes, many things seem to bother Maestro Leonardo and that is most unfortunate. He still does not understand that with the exception of Princess Beatrice, everyone in this town is a servant to the Moor and that it is my responsibility to look after the welfare and security of the duchy. I am not supposed to be the lackey of a repugnant, irreverent, buggering twit whose main preoccupations are the backsides of his boys, painting walls and building a colossal equus caballus.

LUDOVICO: The problem with you is that you don't understand artists. Among all other creatures in the world, artists are the most self-centered, the most arrogant, the most temperamental—

BERNARDINO: I noticed.

LUDOVICO: But they have to be! How else is a man to reach into the depths of his soul for the essence of perfection if he is not totally immersed in himself? It is impossible, especially for a man like Maestro Leonardo. He is a genius, trust me. He is a true genius. No one else could have designed something so—so incredibly awe-inspiring as this horse. I have never seen anything so beautiful in my life. It—it takes my breath away. *(Pause)* Look at those eyes, they are on fire, on fire! Look at the flaring nostrils and at the delicate contour of each limb, the tendons and the muscles! It—it is overwhelming beauty encased in a fistful of clay.

BERNARDINO: *(Aside)* Poetic, perhaps, yet, irrelevant.

LUDOVICO: In any case, it is no use getting excited over the size of the horse anymore than over how much money we have to spend on it. Such displays of choler raise the temperature of the body, upset the bowels and make you ill. I will talk to Maestro Leonardo and see what can be done.

SOUND: A bell rings.

Exit **Bernardino**.

BERNARDINO: *(Off)* You! Seek out the princess and stay in her company! Run back if she steps out of the garden!

Enter **Cecilia**. *She appears from behind the wall.*

LUDOVICO: *(Frightened)* My dearest, what are you doing? Beatrice is in the garden!

CECILIA: And while she's frolicking, playing her girlish, fanciful games, I look after my lover. *(Pause)* Will I see you tonight, or will I be forced to spend another evening looking out the window, telling my woes to the moon, instead of reciting my love to the Moor?

LUDOVICO: My dearest, I am sorry I have neglected you. You don't know how much I think of you. But, alas—

CECILIA: *Alas* has very little do with it, Ludovico. Say, 'but Beatrice,' and I would understand perfectly.

LUDOVICO: How can I ever thank you for being so understanding?

CECILIA: *(Laughs)* You can't.

Enter **Bernardino**.

LUDOVICO: *(To* **Bernardino***)* What is it? *(To* **Cecilia***)* Beatrice is on the way! Please, leave!

CECILIA: And if I don't?

LUDOVICO: Cecilia, please, don't do this to me. I don't need the aggravation. Beatrice—Beatrice has an awful temper.

CECILIA: She is infantile.

LUDOVICO: Yes, she is, my dearest, of course you are right.

CECILIA: Ignore her.

LUDOVICO: Cecilia! Enough. This is unworthy of you! You are behaving like—like Beatrice! Why are you making it so difficult for me?

CECILIA: Because I love you!

LUDOVICO: And I love you. I more than love you, I adore you! Let's do this, go to Vigevano. I will get away for a few days and meet you there. What do you say?

CECILIA: I say it is a ghastly idea. There is nothing to do there but play with the cows and chase sheep. No, my darling. I cannot bear the smell of the country and I refuse to turn into a peasant.

BERNARDINO: *(Warning)* Sire!

LUDOVICO: *(To **Cecilia**)* Fine! Do what you will but now—! Get back to your rooms!

Exit **Cecilia Stage Right**. *Enter* **Beatrice Stage Left**.

LUDOVICO: Here she is! How many did you find?

BEATRICE: How many? How many—what?

LUDOVICO: Butterflies.

BEATRICE: Oh, I lost count at five hundred and fifty. And do you know why I lost count? *(Sweetly)* Because I lost my concentration. And do you know why I lost my concentration? *(Pause)* Because when I raised my eyes to look upon a beautiful, fluttering creature—yellow with blue and red spots that was flying higher than the rest—I caught sight of someone strolling in the portico. It was a person that I think is called Cecilia. Do you know who she is?

Exit **Bernardino**.

BEATRICE: What is that Gallerani woman doing in Milan?

LUDOVICO: My love, please—

BEATRICE: You told me you sent her away!

LUDOVICO: She came back! Amore, please be reasonable!

BEATRICE: *(Softly)* Reasonable! Reasonable! You expect me to be reasonable when you are keeping your mistress in the palace?

LUDOVICO: I am not keeping anyone anywhere. Cecilia is an old friend. I cannot stop her from coming to town.

BEATRICE: *(Screams)* Yes, you can and you will! Oh, to think you allow that old whore here, right under my nose!

LUDOVICO: That is not fair, Beatrice. Cecilia is not a whore and she—she is not old.

BEATRICE: Oh, really? I am sure the bitch is at least twenty years old! How dare you! *(Pause)* What's that smell?

LUDOVICO: Smell?

BEATRICE: Perfume! She was here! That woman–in this room!

LUDOVICO: No, no, no! It—it's Bernardino, he likes to douse himself with strange lotions, takes after the French.

BEATRICE: *(Weeping)* You love her more than you love me!

LUDOVICO: *(Pleads)* Please, don't. It breaks my heart. I adore you, you are my life!

BEATRICE: I am leaving. I am going to my sister in Mantua. I will ask Isabella to find me a place in a nunnery.

LUDOVICO: Don't talk like that! Don't you know what you mean to me? You are the sun that greets me in the morning, the moon that inspires and feeds my passion.

BEATRICE: *(Softly)* No, no, no. I am leaving, I'm going to Mantua.

LUDOVICO: *(Pouting)* What about me? Will you abandon me, will you leave me alone?

BEATRICE: Alone? No. *(Screams)* With Cecilia Gallerani!

LUDOVICO: *(Pause)* Very well, as you wish, my love. I will tell Bernardino to—

BEATRICE: I will tell him! I don't want that—that fawning, crawling worm to misunderstand *my* command!

LUDOVICO: Crawling worm, is it? *(Aside)* Incredible. I am surrounded by malcontents! *(Calls)* Bernardino!

Enter **Bernardino.**

BERNARDINO: Excellency? *(Pause)* My lady?

BEATRICE: Cecilia Gallerani has twenty-four hours to leave the city—and no misunderstandings! *(Sees the statuette)* Oh but what is this? Oh, it is too beautiful for words!

LUDOVICO: Yes—isn't it?

BEATRICE: It is exquisite. But, I love his work. Where is he?

LUDOVICO: Do you want to send for him? I am sure Maestro Leonardo would gladly put aside everything to attend to you, my love.

BEATRICE: Oh, I would never think of imposing on Maestro Leonardo.

BERNARDINO: *(Aside)* Why not? You impose on everyone else.

LUDOVICO: Bernardino?

BERNARDINO: I was saying that Maestro Leonardo is probably working on the wall—a wall on which he has been working for three years.

LUDOVICO: Three years? That long?

BERNARDINO: That long.

LUDOVICO: It is my fault. I keep giving him things to do.

BERNARDINO: True. But, it is also true that Maestro Leonardo loves to experiment and to improvise, something you should not allow, since it is you who pays the bills.

LUDOVICO: Three years. That is a bit too long, I think.

BERNARDINO: Three years. That is a bit too long, I know.

BEATRICE: *(Sweetly)* Is it possible, you think—oh, I know you're going to say no, I know you are!

LUDOVICO: *(Laughing)* What?

BEATRICE: Do you think Maestro Leonardo can come up with something wonderful for me to wear at the ball?

LUDOVICO: The ball? The ball! Oh—

BEATRICE: You forgot?

LUDOVICO: No! I did not forget. Why—why, yes, of course! I mean, what kind of a question is that? Of course he will be delighted to do what he can for you. *(To* **Bernardino***)* I tell you, there is no keeping up with her!

BERNARDINO: *(Aside)* Not at your age.

BEATRICE: I've been thinking, I do not want to be unfair. Perhaps twenty-four hours is not enough time. Tell Cecilia Gallerani that she has thirty hours, thirty hours to leave town. That is more than enough time for her to pack her girdles and wigs. *(Pause)* Oh, well. I'm off, off to spread a little inspiration!

Exit **Beatrice**.

LUDOVICO: Why is it every time she is around I feel like a powerless, bungling fool?

BERNARDINO: Beauty and youth, Your Excellency. It is the irresistible combination that enslaves humankind; it dulls the senses of those not so blessed.

LUDOVICO: *(Pause)* Never mind that. Didn't I tell Cecilia to stay out of sight?

BERNARDINO: You did.

LUDOVICO: And you are my witness!

BERNARDINO: I am.

LUDOVICO: Now, she has made a mess of things. That's it, she has to go. See if among those people you know you can find her a husband—a rich husband, that way it will not cost me anything.

BERNARDINO: A rich husband for Cecilia Gallerani.

LUDOVICO: Unless she wants to go to a nunnery!

BERNARDINO: I will see what I can do.

LUDOVICO: You do that.

BERNARDINO: Anything else, Your Excellency? *(Pause)* Then, I leave you so you can dwell on the fate of—horses.

The counselor bows so low, he tickles the floor with the feather in his hat. Blackout.

Scene vi

Later that night. **Leonardo's** *apartments* .

MACHIAVELLI: You have set yourself up very nicely, my friend.

LEONARDO: We do what we can.

MACHIAVELLI: How big is this place?

LEONARDO: I have five rooms downstairs, including my laboratory–and four–

MACHIAVELLI: A laboratory?

LEONARDO: *(Nods)* It is where I spend hours trying to turn something into something else.

MACHIAVELLI: Like what?

LEONARDO: *(Pause)* Like this.

MACHIAVELLI: What is it?

LEONARDO: It is a chemical solution; pigment blended with beeswax and three other ingredients. When mixed with paint or ink, anything written or drawn fades until–poof–it is no more.

MACHIAVELLI: You mean–

LEONARDO: It disappears.

MACHIAVELLI: I thought artists thrived on eternal recognition. Doesn't your invention defeat the purpose?

LEONARDO: *(Confident smile)* Science is like that; that which seems useless today, may have a purpose tomorrow. *(To **Fra Valentino**)* Brother, you–you have not said two words all night. Have you taken a vow of silence?

FRA VALENTINO: *(Laughs)* No, no. I just–would rather listen and learn.

LEONARDO: Did you hear that, Antonio? Lorenzo–Salai!

MARCO: *I* heard it, Maestro.

LEONARDO: I'm sure you did. *(To **Machiavelli**)* How was supper?

MACHIAVELLI: *(To **Sofia**)* My good woman, Maestro Leonardo was right about you.

SOFIA: Right about me? Well, he's too kind, sir, too kind. He should not bother with the likes of me. *(Pause)* I'm not anything important, unlike my sister.

MACHIAVELLI: *(Smiles)* Your sister is–important?

SOFIA: Oh, yes, sir. She–she associates with royalty.

MACHIAVELLI: You don't say?

SOFIA: I am saying it, sir. She works at the citadel.

MACHIAVELLI: Really?

SOFIA: I don't want you to misunderstand, sir. I love serving Maestro Leonardo. He is a very kind soul. Why, do you know he goes to market, buys as many little birds as they have and instead of bringing them home so I can turn them into a savory stew, he sets them free? He has a veritable heart of gold.

MACHIAVELLI: I know, I know. And tell me, your sister–

SOFIA: My sister? You want to know about Maria?

LEONARDO: *(To* **Machiavelli***)* You don't, really.

MACHIAVELLI: *(Laughs)* But I do!

SOFIA: *(Pause)* Well, Maria is younger than me by ten years, sir, although you would not know it by looking at her. It's her work, see, it tries her so and has turned my sweet, sweet little sister into a worrywart. It is a real pity because she used to be so gay. But, that was before she spent her days fretting about everything and frowning about all.

MACHIAVELLI: Why?

SOFIA: *(Pause)* She works in the kitchen–

MACHIAVELLI: A cook?

SOFIA: No, sir. I wish she was but she is not. *(Pause)* She–she tastes the food before it is served to the Duke and his family. My feeling is she takes it to heart. After all, who would want to poison our dear prince, or his lovely bride? Milan's never been in better hands. People love the Moor and his Beatrice, who, I should add, is the fairest and most beloved of princesses. He–the Moor, that is–he's done wonders for this town.

MACHIAVELLI: *(To* **Leonardo***)* Why is Ludovico called "The Moor?"

LEONARDO: You have never seen him? He's dark–

SOFIA: Oh but not as dark as a Moor, sir. *I* have known a few of *them* and Ludovico is no Moor.

MACHIAVELLI: So you think your sister is safe?

SOFIA: At least from intentional poisoning. I can't answer for bad cooking.

MACHIAVELLI: What do you mean?

SOFIA: Well, about two years ago the Moor employed a Neapolitan braggart to cook at the palace. One day the fellow resolved to get artistic and made liver in a heavy cream sauce of mushrooms, onions and wine. Liver being liver, was not and my poor, sweet Maria became so ill the Duke was convinced she had been poisoned. She got well, yes but not before retching not only the liver, the onions and the mushrooms but parts of her own liver and other stuff as well. The cook–rest his soul–was tortured and hanged the day before Maria was back on her feet. That is why I always say that it is better to cook the goose, than end a cooked goose yourself.

LEONARDO: Salai–

SALAI: Yes, Master?

LEONARDO: Make yourself useful. You too, Lorenzo. Antonio, you and Marco give them a hand, take some of these to the pantry.

SOFIA: I don't need help, Maestro, I am a strong woman and they don't help as much as they interfere.

LEONARDO: Help, please, we need to be alone.

LORENZO: Yes, Maestro.

Exit the boys and **Sofia**. *Pause.*

MACHIAVELLI: A cooked goose! *(Laughs)* Can you imagine the look on the man's face–standing there, a rope tight around his neck, ready to hang? And all because a peasant wench got the runs!

LEONARDO: Enough, please!

FRA VALENTINO: Maestro–

LEONARDO: *(Looks at* **Machiavelli***)* Brother–

FRA VALENTINO: Messer Machiavelli was saying that you are building a monument for the house of Sforza–a monument to end all monuments.

LEONARDO: I don't know about that.

He picks out a drawing from the back and spreads it on the table.

FRA VALENTINO: A horse?

LEONARDO: With Francesco Sforza–the Duke's father, on the saddle.

MACHIAVELLI: I heard it is–

LEONARDO: –big. Ludovico said it had to be spectacular–well, it is. *(Pause)* Now, my friend. Are you going to tell what brings you and Fra Valentino to Milan?

MACHIAVELLI: *I* came to see you–

LEONARDO: I am so glad you did–

MACHIAVELLI: –and Fra Valentino came to ask Ludovico for money. I warned him that it is easier to pull a tooth from a crocodile, than it is to get money from royalty.

LEONARDO: True.

FRA VALENTINO: *(Haltingly)* It–it is for a worthy cause.

MACHIAVELLI: *(To* **Leonardo***)* He wants to build a school–

FRA VALENTINO: *(Pause-softly)* Yes. We–we want to build a school behind San Giovanni–

LEONARDO: San Giovanni? *(Looks at* **Machiavelli***)* I don't remember a San Giovanni in Florence.

FRA VALENTINO: San Giovanni in Bergamo.

LEONARDO: *(Surprised)* Bergamo? *(To* **Machiavelli***)* I don't understand–you come from Florence and he's from Bergamo–how did you two–

MACHIAVELLI: Who said I came from Florence?

LEONARDO: Oh.

FRA VALENTINO: You see, back home, we are trying to teach the children–not the children of the rich, mind you but the boys and girls of the poor–teach them to read and write. We feel it is a sin to doom generations of our children–our most precious resource– to ignorance. How can we allow them to grow up without ever aspiring to a future? *(Pause)* A person can only aspire to a future, as long as they have hope and you can only hope if you are enlightened. *(Pause)* Our problem is that we are a poor village and education, it seems, is only for those born into wealth. But, what then, of the hundreds of thousands of peasant children from poor families who will someday inherit this country? What is the future of Italy if its children cannot read and write? My–our arguments do not impress our superiors and we are finding it more and more difficult to continue our work. *(Sad smile)* It is as if the Church was the exclusive holding of the privileged. That cannot be, it just cannot be allowed. The Church must struggle for the truth, for impartiality and justice. *(Pause)* I'm sorry, I'm blabbering nonsense.

LEONARDO: No, no, no–

FRA VALENTINO: Well, I thought, then, why not ask the Moor for help?

MACHIAVELLI: *(To **Leonardo**)* I told him that it is not in the interest of royalty to raise the poor from ignorance.

FRA VALENTINO: We must try! We must follow our conscience. A man who does not follow his conscience negates the most divine gift our Lord and Heavenly Master has provided for us, reason!

MACHIAVELLI: Wonderful sentiment but, I'm afraid you are wasting your time.

FRA VALENTINO: We wrote several letters to the Duke, without a reply, so I decided to make my case in person. *(Pause)* So far, I have not even been allowed inside the citadel.

MACHIAVELLI: *(To **Leonardo**)* –that is when I mentioned your name.

LEONARDO: Me?

MACHIAVELLI: I told him that my friend–the most prodigious artist in the world–the great Leonardo, works for the Duke of Milan and that I was sure you would be gracious enough to afford an introduction. *(Pause)* I know it is an imposition on our part–

LEONARDO: No, it is not–

MACHIAVELLI: –being that you are so busy, with the equestrian monument and building arms for the Moor–

LEONARDO: *(Taken back)* Alms for the poor?

MACHIAVELLI: No, not "alms for the poor." Arms for the Moor, you know, guns and things–weapons.

LEONARDO: Who told you that?

MACHIAVELLI: Is it true?

LEONARDO: *(Pause)* Yes and no. I've been designing weapons for years.

MACHIAVELLI: You have?

LEONARDO: Oh, yes, since I was a boy. *(Pause)* I offered them to Ludovico; wrote him a long letter of what my weapons could do but–he is not interested. Pity. They–my weapons would give him an incredible advantage in war.

MACHIAVELLI: Why waste your time on Ludovico? The French are ready to pounce on Milan. When they do, he will be out of a duchy and you will be out of a job. You better look out for yourself, my friend. Ludovico does not have much time left.

LEONARDO: I hope you're wrong. I don't know if you know this–no reason why you should–but I left Florence a nobody. The Moor received me with opened arms, gave me work and more than work, he has allowed me the freedom to grow. *(Lowers his voice)* I have complete run of the dungeons at the citadel–even made friends with the executioners–they let me work on the bodies–

MACHIAVELLI: Work– *(Pause)* What is it you do?

LEONARDO: *(Matter-of-factly)* I dissect them, to make anatomical drawings.

MACHIAVELLI: *(Feigning alarm)* You have become a ghoul?

LEONARDO: A scientist! No one has ever done it before. *(Pause)* Yes, everything I have–this house, my position at court, I owe to Ludovico. It is true that sometimes I don't get paid for months, that I waste time painting walls, building monuments and even–would you believe it–designing girdles for the princess but he makes up for it–in his own way. He is a dear man, an unpretentious, gentle soul who delights in music, art and poetry. *(Pause)* I like him. He does not have the genius to repress and murder his subjects, like some others in this crazy country of ours.

MACHIAVELLI: And what others might you be talking about?

LEONARDO: Take your pick; depends on what part of the country you are in. In Florence you have the Medicis; in Rome–well, the Borgias really are in a league of their own; beginning with that murdering beast Çesare, who killed his brother–his own brother– to satisfy his blood-lust for power!

MACHIAVELLI: Really?

LEONARDO: Yes, really. Çesare Borgia is a conquering despot, the personification of evil.

MACHIAVELLI: *(Sarcastic)* But, Maestro, Çesare Borgia is a prince of the Church!

LEONARDO: Have you ever heard anything so bizarre? *(Pause)* And why not? His father is the Pope! His Holiness Alexander VI, Vicar of Rome–nothing but a Spanish maggot with a taste for his own daughter!

MACHIAVELLI: Maestro!

LEONARDO: *(Pause)* Oh, dear–please forgive me, brother. I have no business–

FRA VALENTINO: I am a simple man, Maestro. I do not involve myself in politics.

LEONARDO: And that is exactly my point. You and the hundreds of thousands of honest, hardworking, loving members of the clergy–you *are* the church–not this soldier-politician sitting on the throne of Peter.

MACHIAVELLI: Leonardo, these weapons of yours, are they secret?

LEONARDO: How can they be secret if you know about them? Take a look.

MACHIAVELLI: What's this?

LEONARDO: A flying machine.

FRA VALENTINO: How ingenious! *(Pause)* Does it–fly?

LEONARDO: Not yet. *(Pause)* This is a hollow, cylindrical shaft with fins, that you fill with explosives and shoot from a small cannon.

MACHIAVELLI: Why the fins?

LEONARDO: Aerial stability.

MACHIAVELLI: If you say so.

LEONARDO: *(Points)* That is an armored car with protruding guns that fire at long range. The drawing next to it are two versions of a mechanical scythe on wheels that when pulled by a horse, will cut down the enemy.

MACHIAVELLI: Wouldn't the horse risk being chopped up as well?

LEONARDO: *(Pause)* I am still working on it.

MACHIAVELLI: Ah, this I recognize–

LEONARDO: Yes. It is a giant crossbow. It takes several dozen men to load it with giant arrows.

MACHIAVELLI: Haven't you heard? Arrows are outdated.

LEONARDO: As I said–

MACHIAVELLI: *(Chuckles)* You are still working on it. *(Pause)* And what is that?

LEONARDO: An underwater boat.

FRA VALENTINO: A what?

LEONARDO: A boat designed to pop to the surface from the bottom of the sea, to destroy unsuspecting enemy ships.

MACHIAVELLI: To me, a boat underwater, is a boat that's been sunk.

LEONARDO: That's the problem with you politicians, you have no imagination, you are too practical!

MACHIAVELLI: Is that what you call it? *(Pause)* Let me ask you. Have you–have you built any of these?

LEONARDO: No. *(Pause)* Can you guess what this is?

MACHIAVELLI: I don't have a clue.

LEONARDO: It is a gun but not just any gun, it shoots projectiles in great numbers, one after another, at incredible speed, raining death on the enemy. If mounted on a turret, this gun can destroy a legion in minutes. Are you impressed?

MACHIAVELLI: Overwhelmed.

LEONARDO: It is a shame. If built, these weapons–my weapons– would prove the most lethal arsenal in the world, perhaps revolutionize warfare, maybe, who knows, they would eliminate war altogether.

MACHIAVELLI: You notice, brother, that my friend here, is full of contradictions. He does not eat meat but does not mind to dissect the dead. He rants against the ravages and brutality of war and yet, he has a consuming interest in weapons of mass destruction. *(Pause)* And let's not forget that I have seen this gentle fellow, whose long, delicate fingers are the fine tools of an artist, beat the–life out of two burly brutes–stonemasons, I believe they were–by himself!

FRA VALENTINO: *(Pause)* Why do you say that these weapons would eliminate war?

LEONARDO: They would only have to be used once. After that, the news will spread and I guarantee there would not be a prince, duke, or soldier who would dare face them again. In other words, these are tools, not of death but for political manipulation. As soon as a state is threatened with invasion, its army would be demoralized and surrender rather than face annihilation.

MACHIAVELLI: Far from eliminating war, what these machines would do–assuming they work–is allow the highest bidder to conquer with ease and rule by force. A very dangerous proposition, Maestro. *(Pause)* And one that could get you in a lot of trouble.

LEONARDO: *(Pause)* Why?

MACHIAVELLI: Because, if word gets out that you have been hired–say by Ludovico–to build extraordinary weapons, giving him superiority in the field–his enemies would be wise to assassinate you.

LEONARDO: *(Pause)* I never thought about that.

MACHIAVELLI: My advice to you is, keep your interest in the military to yourself.

LEONARDO: *(Pause)* Well, there are no weapons, so no one should feel threatened. *(Pause)* Fra Valentino? *(Pause)* Would you mind terribly if I drew your likeness? It will not take long, I promise.

FRA VALENTINO: Why?

LEONARDO: It is for–for a picture I am working on.

MACHIAVELLI: Let me guess–for the wall?

FRA VALENTINO: If it would help you.

LEONARDO: *(Calls)* Lorenzo!

MACHIAVELLI: I noticed two faces missing on your fresco.

LEONARDO: Christ and the betrayer.

FRA VALENTINO: *(Frowns)* Dear me. As man of God, the thought of representing my divine and gracious Lord is enough to give me pause but, the Judas?

LEONARDO: You need not fear, brother. You possess a sense of duty, a selfless devotion to your fellow man that is perfectly Christ-like! To speak the truth, I am tempted to ask you to walk across the public baths.

Enter the boys.

LORENZO: Yes, Maestro?

LEONARDO: Notebook and pencil! Quick!

*Exit **Lorenzo**.*

LEONARDO: Niccòlo, do you know what I heard?

MACHIAVELLI: I cannot imagine. You hear many things.

LEONARDO: Someone told me that you are working for the Republic.

MACHIAVELLI: I am in the ruling Consiglio, yes.

*Enter **Lorenzo**. He gives **Leonardo** his notebook and pencils.*

LEONARDO: Thank you. That will be all.

*Exit **Lorenzo** and the boys.*

LEONARDO: *(To* **Machiavelli***)* Is that why you've traveled so far to see me? Is Florence worried about Ludovico?

MACHIAVELLI: *(Laughs)* No. Florence has more serious things to worry about.

LEONARDO: Savonarola?

MACHIAVELLI: Savonarola. *(Pause)* You know the difference between us, Leonardo? You are too–how shall I say–too gullible. You believe every piece of gossip you hear and worse, you repeat that same nonsense without taking time to find out if it's true or not. I guess your naivete goes hand in hand with your vocation, yes? As an artist something catches your eye, you take pencil to paper and draw its outward likeness, glossing over what is most important, its underlying substance. For instance, here we have our good brother, Fra Valentino, whom you scarcely met this morning. Fra Valentino is a good looking and intelligent fellow who has charmed you into making you think he is endowed with the loving grace of a true man of God. So much in fact, that you have decided to use him as a model for your Christ, although you know nothing about him except what he's told you and what he's told you is no more and no less than what he wants you to know about him.

LEONARDO: My celebrated compatriot, there are people who look at the blue sky and think, "What a beautiful day" Not you. You look at the sky and wonder how long before it clouds up and starts to rain.

MACHIAVELLI: Because thunderstorms can gather in the blink of an eye and I don't like to be caught off-guard. So, I find shelter whereas you–you stand in the middle of the piazza, hoping the inclement weather goes away while lighting bolts crash around you to the accompaniment of reverberating thunder. *(Pause)* Another thing, not only do you believe everything you hear on the street, you are easily swayed–impressed is a better word–by the ruling class. I, on the other hand, am not fooled by looks, certainly not by the gold-laden embroidery of a fine dress, by official seals, not even by proclamations of divine guidance. I have met princes, dukes, priests and Popes who, after half an hour, I understood were nothing but parasites. I have also met wretched paupers who could have taught the princes, dukes, priests and Popes a thing or two. It is, you see, my firm conviction that in order to know a man

MACHIAVELLI: *(Cont.)* –one must peel every layer of lies, half-truths and pretense before the true self is exposed. Let me give you another example. Your boy–

LEONARDO: *(Looks up from the drawing)* I'm sorry?

MACHIAVELLI: That boy of yours. The one with yellow hair.

LEONARDO: Salai?

MACHIAVELLI: Yes.

LEONARDO: What about him? *(To* **Fra Valentino***)* Brother, will you please turn your head this way a little more–that's it! Perfect. Don't move.

MACHIAVELLI: I can tell he is your favorite. *(Pause)* Quite a little angel–like those you like to paint and–*do* so well. *(Pause)* Where did you find him?

LEONARDO: Find him?

MACHIAVELLI: Yes– *(Teasing)* The truth, now.

LEONARDO: Why?

MACHIAVELLI: I'm curious. Where did you find your–precious Salai? That's not his real name, is it?

LEONARDO: *(Pause)* His name is Giacomo. I found him roaming the streets–four years ago, on Santa Maria Magdalena's day. His father was being executed in the piazza–

MACHIAVELLI: How interesting.

LEONARDO: –hanged for robbing the sacristy.

MACHIAVELLI: And you were cheering as the drop went–plop?

LEONARDO: I'd been engaged to sketch the hanging.

MACHIAVELLI: Ah–

LEONARDO: *(Pause)* And–well, there I was, pencil in hand, drawing–

MACHIAVELLI: Like now–

LEONARDO: –making careful notes, when I noticed a small hand trying to relieve me of my purse. Salai was ten. I grabbed him and was tempted to have him participate first hand in the drama unfolding before us when to my surprise, I found out that the man swinging by the neck in the piazza was his very own papa. I think stealing was Salai's way to commemorate his father's passing. He's been with me ever since. He's a good boy.

MACHIAVELLI: His father was a thief and heaven only knows what the mother was like. That boy was probably born in a rat infested hell-hole where he crawled among human waste until he

MACHIAVELLI: *(Cont.)* –was old enough to go out in the world to beg and plunder. There are many ways to change someone like Salai and they all entail having him meet his maker. Nothing will change him, not new clothes; food; a roof over his head; kind words, or the fear of hell will make a difference.

LEONARDO: You don't know the boy as I do.

MACHIAVELLI: *(Smiles)* Why don't you put him in care of the brothers?

LEONARDO: Salai is fine where he is. He's a sensitive and caring child.

MACHIAVELLI: And so was his father and the thousands of dregs we step over and avoid in our glorious city streets. You hope he has turned from gallows prey to altar boy. He'll look at you with those big blue eyes and convince you he has changed, when in fact he has become a better thief and a more persuasive liar! Leonardo, the world is a vicious circle of weakness and failing. When are you going to understand that simple truth? It's evil breeding evil. *(Pause)* To look at him sitting there, a stranger walking in might have thought that Salai was a heavenly creature sent to earth by the Trinity to announce a miracle. Give him a pair of wings and a halo and voila! Salai becomes everything an angel should be–and then some. Yes, no one would ever think of Salai as anything but the purest and most chaste representative of childhood innocence. But is he? Or is there something else behind the lovely blue eyes, long lashes and the blond curls?

LEONARDO: Finished! *(Shows the picture to **Fra Valentino**)* What do you think?

FRA VALENTINO: It is–excellent!

MACHIAVELLI: Maestro, keep in mind that men of the cloth rarely look at themselves in the mirror. I suggest you ask for my opinion.

LEONARDO: Oh, for crying out loud, Niccòlo! What is the matter with you, today?

MACHIAVELLI: *(Looking at the picture)* I like to be contrary. You know that. *(Pause)* Very good. Brother, it is my humble opinion that you never looked better. You could say you're on your way to immortality. *(Pause)* Now Leonardo, do you remember what happened this morning?

LEONARDO: Stop, please. You are giving me a headache.

MACHIAVELLI: I was leaving the refectory when your precious Salai crashed into me. Later, as I walked out of the monastery, I found my purse was missing. Coincidence? Perhaps. Only thing is, I have a habit of never losing anything. I also always carry two purses at the same time, one in front with very little change–to frustrate pickpockets–and one behind my back, with the rest of my money. If, in fact Salai picked my purse, he is very, very good; he is a supremely skilled young thief and there is something to be said for that. And of course, there is no law that says that an angel cannot have sticky fingers. The point is this, it is possible that Salai is the perfect altar boy who delights priests with his charming smile and lovely innocence but who lies when he says good morning and steals away the Eucharist. Just like it's possible that a seemingly benevolent ruler like Ludovico Sforza is also a vile, wicked tyrant. So, be warned. Remember that given fair warning, only those that are deaf die when hostilities break out. *(Pause)* Fra Valentino–don't you think we should be going?

LEONARDO: Why? It is still early.

MACHIAVELLI: Not early enough. We–have a long trip ahead of us. Thank you for a very entertaining evening. You are a most gracious host.

LEONARDO: I thought Fra Valentino needed an introduction to the Duke?

FRA VALENTINO: Oh but I do. *(Pause)* It's just that–I have already been gone too long.

MACHIAVELLI: Mention it to the Moor, see what he says, then–send word to Fra Valentino–

FRA VALENTINO: At San Giovanni, in Bergamo.

MACHIAVELLI: Goodnight, Leonardo.

FRA VALENTINO: Yes and thank you so much.

LEONARDO: I am the one who should thank you, brother.

MACHIAVELLI: Oh, by the way– *(Aside)* About that boy of yours–no need to be upset. I was only illustrating a point.

Exit **Machiavelli** *and* **Fra Valentino**.

LEONARDO: *(Ponders)* An angel with sticky fingers. *(Pause)* Giacomo! Salai!

Enter **Salai**.

SALAI: They left?
LEONARDO: Yes.

Salai *slowly makes his way to* **Leonardo** *and sits on his lap.*

SALAI: He was staring at me.
LEONARDO: Was he, now? *(Pause)* If it were someone else, I'd say he was enticed by your curls–certainly not by your charm. But Machiavelli–he has a predilection for whores of the opposite sex.
SALAI: How do you know?
LEONARDO: Because I have known him since he was a boy.
SALAI: Was he your lover?
LEONARDO: *(Laughs)* God forbid! He was the most homely looking boy I ever saw. No, my father did some work for his mother–
SALAI: What?
LEONARDO: Lawyer work–I think her husband beat her. I was twenty-seven. Niccòlo was ten.
SALAI: *(Surprised)* You're older than he is?
LEONARDO: *(Laughs)* Considerably.
SALAI: He looks–like an old man!
LEONARDO: It's all that worry etched on his face–he's worries about everything, never gives his mind a rest.
SALAI: He's creepy.
LEONARDO: Now, that's unfair–especially after all the nice things he said about you.
SALAI: He did?
LEONARDO: Yes. He thinks you are a very talented–pretty and angelic looking–little thief. *(Softly)* He said you stole his purse.
SALAI: *(Indignant)* That's–that's not true!
LEONARDO: So why did you run into him, at the refectory.
SALAI: W–why?
LEONARDO: Are you back to your old tricks? *(Pause)* Where are you getting money for candy? I smelled candy on your breath this morning.
SALAI: Tomassino gave it to me.
LEONARDO: Really? Who is Tomassino and what is this Tomassino doing giving you candy?

SALAI: *(Cries)* I did not steal anything! I swore–I said I was never going to steal again! *(Pause)* You said you would trust me.

LEONARDO: Trust you? Why did you run into Machiavelli?

SALAI: It was an accident!

LEONARDO: An accident–

SALAI: *Maestro–(Pause)* Do you love me?

Leonardo *answers by kissing the boy on the neck.*

SALAI: I said, do you love me?

Leonardo *outlines the boy's mouth with his finger.*

LEONARDO: You live with me. I taught you to read and write. I taught you to draw. I buy you clothes–

SALAI: But do you love me!?

LEONARDO: I take you everywhere with me–

SALAI: And the others too. Marco, Antonio and Lorenzo–and they too come in your bed, I know they do! *(Pause)* Do you love me or do you love Marco? Do you love me or do you love Lorenzo? Do you love me or do you love Antonio?

LEONARDO: What is it with you?

SALAI: *(Crying)* Last year, you sent me to Messer Fabio with a note. In that note you said 'I'm sending you my student Salai.' In the letter I delivered for you this morning, you said, 'Please give my servant Salai–' *(Pause)* What am I? Your student, your servant? Your whore?

LEONARDO: You are tired.

SALAI: *Do* you love me?

Exit **Salai.**

Leonardo *looks after the boy. He drinks the last of the wine.*

Lights *dim slowly to blackout.*

Scene vii

*Next day. The refectory . **Leonardo** is on the scaffold, working on the fresco. The boys help him. Pause.*

SOUND: The friars singing in the background.

LEONARDO: Are we ready?

LORENZO: I'm ready, Maestro.

LEONARDO: *(Angry)* What is that?

LORENZO: What?

LEONARDO: *(Points to the fresco)* That–that spot on John's cheek! *(Pause)* Who told you, you could give him a birthmark? How dare you!

LORENZO: Me? I–*(Pause)* It's a mosquito.

MARCO: *(Laughs)* A mosquito! The picture is so real, it fooled the bloodsucker and got stuck in the goo!

LEONARDO: Shut up!

MARCO: Yes, Maestro.

*Pause **Leonardo** retouches the painting. Marco climbs the scaffold with a bowl of pigment.*

LEONARDO: What color is this?

LORENZO: Errr–

LEONARDO: I asked for aquamarine! So why am I dipping my brush in blue and not aquamarine! Can't you do anything right? What's the matter with you?

LORENZO: I told Marco–

LEONARDO: Marco!?

MARCO: Yes, Master?

LEONARDO: I'm not talking to you! *(To **Lorenzo**)* Who is on the scaffold? Only you and me, right? And if you are up here, at my side, it is because you have the high and mighty privilege to be my assistant. That means you have to know exactly what it is I need, so when I ask you for aquamarine, you give me aquamarine and not yellow–aquamarine and not red–aquamarine and not green!

LEONARDO: *(Cont.)* You would think that after three years you would know aquamarine from the rest of the colors of the rainbow!

LORENZO: I am sorry, Maestro.

LEONARDO: That is not good enough! *(Pause)* Marco–

ANTONIO: *(To **Marco**)* He's in a shit mood, isn't he.

MARCO: *(Points to **Salai**)* His fault.

Salai *sees his friends talking about him and gives them the finger.* **Marco** *blows a kiss his way, then, grabs his crotch as if to say, "have some of this!"*

LEONARDO: *(Screams)* Marco!

MARCO: Yes, Master!

LEONARDO: Wake up!

MARCO: Y–yes, Master.

LEONARDO: Oh, what's the use! I'm surrounded by dilettantes, I'm overwhelmed by fools and clowns! *(Pause)* Why a fresco? Why not something simple–wonderful on canvas? The brothers could hang it on the wall, carry it on their heads as penitence, for all I care! I will tell you this much, in a year or two you won't recognize anything! It will peel and crack. The colors that are so alive now, up on that wall, will no longer vibrate in the light. The tablecloth will fade and lose its patterns and you will not be able to appreciate anything. All because they insisted on a fresco! Fresco painting is for amateurs! *(Pause)* Friars, frescos! Arghhhh!

Enter **Bandello**.

BANDELLO: I don't understand anything anymore.

LEONARDO: What is it you do not understand? Tell us please, brother, don't keep us in suspense. What is it? An intricate mathematical formula, perhaps? A simple expression of devotion from a non-believer?

BANDELLO: Is it perhaps, I am missing something?

LEONARDO: Could be.

BANDELLO: Maybe there is something wrong with my eyes.

LEONARDO: Quite possible, quite possible, indeed.

BANDELLO: It doesn't matter, does it?

LEONARDO: What?

BANDELLO: What time of year, what month, what hour of what day, every time I look up at that wall nothing is changed.

LEONARDO: Of course there is change!

BANDELLO: Where?

LEONARDO: Where?

BANDELLO: Show me. I beg you to tell me, to show me what has changed in the picture from a week ago? *(Pause)* No, let us not be so demanding, no! Pray, tell me what has changed in the last six months? In the last year!?

LEONARDO: A week ago, this half loaf of bread was an apple, not a biblical interpretation but then again, my apprentice is not a scholar.

LORENZO: How was I supposed to—

LEONARDO: —which of course, had to be erased and properly illustrated. Then there is Thomas' pointing finger, it has been cut in half.

ANTONIO: Maestro, the fish!

LEONARDO: Ah, of course, the fish, yes. Two weeks ago I filled the plate in front of Peter and Andrew with fish, here— *(Points)* —to call attention to their trade as fishermen. So, as you can see, brother—

BANDELLO: That is all?

LEONARDO: I do not know why I try, I really don't! You do not understand and there is no hope you ever will and so I ask myself what in Heaven's name I'm doing here! Do me a favor and go away! As if I did not have enough! Let me explain something to you, my dear! Many are a time when you are kneeling comfortably in blissful meditation in the sanctity of the chapel, your melancholy eyes pointing languidly at the blessed Mother while I am either mounting scaffolds or climbing a giant horse's ass!

BANDELLO: And for the last two and a half years, I've had to provide other dining facilities for an entire congregation of friars! You're supposed to be a creative genius, a master artist, a man endowed with supernatural talents—well use your imagination!

LEONARDO: Imagination? Is that what you said?

BANDELLO: Make them up, please I beg you! Be merciful!

LEONARDO: Are you saying that I should– *(Pause)* Boys, pick up your things, we are leaving.

BANDELLO: What do you mean you are leaving?

LEONARDO: It's obvious we are no longer needed, it was to be expected. I am glad, in a way. Now, I can dedicate all my time to the horse, which seems to appreciate our talents more than you do!

BANDELLO: But–you cannot do that!

LEONARDO: *(To* **Antonio***)* There he goes once again telling me what I can and cannot do! Lorenzo, are you ready?

LORENZO: Yes, Maestro.

BANDELLO: Maestro Leonardo, please, you don't understand!

LEONARDO: And now he tells me I don't understand! Antonio?

ANTONIO: Yes, sir!

BANDELLO: I beg you!

LEONARDO: Marco? You have your box?

MARCO: Yes, Maestro.

BANDELLO: Maestro Leonardo, please forgive me!

LEONARDO: Oh, I do. That is why I will not say anything to the Moor. I will let *you* tell his Excellency that I am no longer working on *the Cenacolo*; that I left furious after you had the brazen, crass, bold impertinent gall to suggest that– *(Pause)* Most likely the Moor will toss you in a dungeon so you will never bother with the likes of me.

BANDELLO: Merciful God! Nobody can finish the fresco, no one but the great Leonardo!

LEONARDO: You are wrong, brother, you can. Use your imagination!

BANDELLO: I was wrong.

LEONARDO: Really?

BANDELLO: Yes, yes!

LEONARDO: Doesn't matter. I am still leaving.

BANDELLO: No!!!

LEONARDO: Why can't you leave me alone–tell the abbot to mind his own business. I will finish when I finish, not a second before, not a second after. And not you, nor the abbot–not even our beloved Moor is going to interfere with my work!

Bandello *takes* **Leonardo's** *hand and kisses it.*

LEONARDO: No, come–stop that. Come, come, now. *(Pause)* Look, you don't think that I enjoy having to come here day after day–that somehow I'm prolonging this agony–because that's what painting that wall has become for me, agony pure and simple–you don't think I'm doing it on purpose, do you? Because trust me when I tell you that I am as desperate to finish as you are for me to leave. Yet, I will not be intimidated, pressured or humiliated. It will not do! The wall will be finished when I say it is finished, not a second before and not a second after and there is nothing you or anyone else can do about it. Also, you'd be wise to keep in mind that every minute I waste on your nonsense is time not spent on the wall! As a matter of fact, I was going to fill in the Christ when you came in!"

BANDELLO: *(Softly)* You–you found the Nazarene?

LEONARDO: Well–not *the* Nazarene but a good likeness.

BANDELLO: Oh, that *is* wonderful news, indeed! *(Pause)* What about the Judas? You will have to go on your merry way to hell before you find someone like that. Not–not that I am suggesting you do.

LEONARDO: If need be. What else?

BANDELLO: Nothing.

Exit **Bandello**, **Stage Right**.

Enter **Beatrice** *and* **Silveria**, **Stage Left**.

LEONARDO: My lady!

BEATRICE: I hope we are not disturbing you, Maestro.

LEONARDO: That is impossible. Salai, a chair–quickly!

BEATRICE: No, no, Maestro, I beg you, I can't stay long. *(Pause)* I just dropped by to say how much we have missed you at court.

LEONARDO: Ah, yes–a situation I hope soon to correct. But, for now, I am indebted to your illustrious husband who has seen it in his noble heart to bestowed upon us such favors as would engage us for the next century and a half.

BEATRICE: *(Laughs)* Maestro, I need your advice. *(Pause)* We are having a masked ball and I have nothing to wear!

LEONARDO: *(Forcing a smile)* Is there a particular theme attached to the–entertainment?

BEATRICE: No. That is why I came to you.

LEONARDO: *(Pause)* I have several designs, wonderful styles that were never used in The Feast of Paradise–you remember The Feast of Paradise?

BEATRICE: Oh, yes! It was spectacular!

LEONARDO: You will love my costumes. They represent Spring and its flora. That way, you, my lady, can dress as a rose while his most magnificent Excellency, Ludovico, can dress like a bee. Of course– *(Softly)* –the Moor will have to spend the night buzzing you!

BEATRICE: Oh, that is perfect–perfectly wonderful, Maestro Leonardo! Oh, I don't know what I would do without you! *(Pause)* Wait–if he does that, I'll get dizzy!

LEONARDO: You can always blame it on the wine.

BEATRICE: You are awful!

LEONARDO: I'll come by tomorrow, at four. I'll bring what I have and you choose what you will.

BEATRICE: Thank you, Maestro! *(Pause)* Oh, Silveria, look! Isn't it splendid?

SILVERIA: It's big.

BEATRICE: Maestro–those two empty spots–you know, on the wall, are they on purpose?

LEONARDO: *(Pause)* No.

BEATRICE: Oh. *(Pause)* Well, I am sure you know what to do and I have no doubt my husband will be very pleased.

Exit **Beatrice** *and* **Silveria**.

BEATRICE: *(Off)* Goodbye, Maestro!

LEONARDO: *(Angry)* How can I finish? How can they expect me to, when they will not leave me alone! I have to get out of here! This place is beginning to affect my mind! Do yourselves a favor, clean this mess.

ANTONIO: Where are you going?

LEONARDO: To hell!

Blackout.

Scene viii

Same time. The Vatican. **The Pope's** *study . His Holiness sits on his throne. In the room are several cardinals, including* **Ascanio Cardinal Sforza**.

CARDINAL SFORZA: At this moment–foreign troops are amassing at the border, ready to invade, willing to trample the fatherland; French troops, barbarians, who at any moment will ravage and defile our glorious heritage, loot every town in their path and murder thousands of *our* countrymen. This is infamy, my reverent brothers, this is sacrilege, this is an insult, this is an outrage, this is disgusting and this is evil!

THE POPE: *(Yawns)* But–*this* is not an invasion, it is an incursion. Louis is just fulfilling his promise to help Prince Borgia crush the rebellion in the papal states.

CARDINAL SFORZA: I beg your pardon, Holiness but it is our understanding that in addition to the supply of troops for Prince Borgia, Louis is to march into Milan. Why? What does Milan have to do with the Romagna?

THE POPE: *(Gently)* The Duchy of Milan stands between the French-Italian border and the Romagna, yes? Or is it perhaps we have been misinformed as to the exact location of Lombardy? Then, there is the very delicate matter of who, in fact, owns the title to the Duchy. You cannot deny that King Louis has a legitimate claim–

CARDINAL SFORZA: I deny! I deny! I deny! I deny!

THE POPE: One denial would have sufficed, brother.

CARDINAL SFORZA: Ludovico is the lawful Duke of Milan. The title was awarded by the Holy Roman Emperor Maximilian himself.

THE POPE: Without consulting the Holy See. We've always said that these Holy Roman Emperors are going to be the end of us all with their ill-advised meddling.

CARDINAL SFORZA: *(Very agitated)* Holiness, by my oath, no one but Ludovico Sforza has a claim on Milan!

THE POPE: That, my dear brother, is in dispute.

CARDINAL SFORZA: Holiness, with all due respect, an *Italian* Pope, would never allow this–criminal intrusion of our motherland!

THE POPE: See what I mean, brothers? You noticed the deliberate inflection on *Italian*! *(Pause)* Does he intend to hurl more insults at our person, our family and at this holiest of institutions? *(Pause-to* **Cardinal Sforza***)* Should we point out to our esteemed brother that inviting the French to spend their holidays in Italy has been a tradition of the *Italian* Popes for generations? We recall that in 1266 our venerated ancestor Pope Urban IV offered the Kingdom of Naples to Charles, Duke of Anjou as a reward for protecting the papacy against the German kings. *(Pause)* Pope Urban *was* Italian. *(Pause)* In 1482 Pope Sixtus IV, at odds with Naples and following the precedent established by Pope Urban, offered the kingdom of Naples to King Louis XI of France, which, said Sixtus, belonged to Louis. Sixtus *was* Italian. *(Pause)* And just a few years ago, our esteemed predecessor Innocent VIII again offered Naples to another Charles of France, Charles VIII, if Charles would 'just take it.' Pope Innocent *was* Italian! *(Pause)* We were the ones who forbade *that* Charles, on pain of excommunication, to march on Italy! As you can see, dearest brother, for generations, Italians, not the English, not the Germans and certainly not the Spaniards, have been opening doors to barbarians! We live in dangerous times, brother and if we have bruised your princely sensitivities, it is because we cannot forget that it was your own brother, Ludovico Sforza, Duke of Milan who gave King Charles of France free passage through his territories, to invade Naples. Why? Because the Moor thought Naples was planning to invade Milan! He was wrong! And not only was our esteemed Ludovico wrong but that French invasion triggered what we now call "the Italian Wars!" *(Pause)* Still, we are impartial. Our goal is and has always been the peace of the world and the well being of the Apostolic See. That is and should be our only concern. We are willing to travel to Milan and mediate this unholy dissension between Duke Sforza and King Louis of France. Lest we forget, we are messengers of our redeemer, the Prince of Peace and our quest for peace is never-ending! *(Pause)* Of course, security for our journey will be guaranteed by the commander of the Papal Troops– *(Enter* **Çesare***)* His Eminence, Çesare Cardinal Borgia.

Blackout.

Scene ix

Same time. The citadel; **Ludovico's** *study . He and* **Bernardino**, *look at a map.*

BERNARDINO: There will be no more than two-hundred fifty troops traveling with the Pope, including Çesare Borgia's fifty bodyguards. *(Pause)* You, on the other hand, have the most powerful army in Italy. There are fifteen thousand of the best fed, best equipped and best paid soldiers in the continent, including a thousand lancers, every one of them under the expert command of Galeazzo di San Severino, the most renown, learned and feared General of our age. In addition, the ducal troops are encamped outside and around the city, creating an insurmountable defensive shield. So, to attack Milan—in my view—is to commit suicide. That said, it is never a good idea to underestimate the recklessness of kings, especially French kings.

LUDOVICO: Extraordinary.

BERNARDINO: What is?

LUDOVICO: That his Holiness is traveling with so few men, Çesare is known never to travel without half his army.

BERNARDINO: His Holiness is coming on a mission of peace; more soldiers would provoke distrust.

LUDOVICO: *(Pause)* Consider this—Çesare and the Pope are traveling together; you take one, you take the other. With one stroke, you rid Italy of both. *(Pause)* I will ride out to receive and welcome the Pope. His troops will not be allowed to enter Milan's sovereign territory, of course, only a minimum number of bodyguards. *(Pause)* Let's have the papal procession end at the Grazie; he can witness the unveiling of the—

BERNARDINO: Excellency, the fresco is not finished and from what I've heard, it will take another ten years. The Pope travels to Milan next week.

LUDOVICO: Maestro Leonardo will have to hurry, now, won't he? *(Pause)* And while his Holiness is busy touring the city, General di San Severino will surround the papal troops outside the city gates, disarm them and take them prisoners. Once his Holiness is cut off from his men, he and his bastard son will be at my mercy.

LUDOVICO: *(Cont.)* I think that General San Severino can neutralize two-hundred men?

BERNARDINO: Fifteen thousand against two-hundred—the odds are certainly in his favor.

LUDOVICO: *(Irony)* That's what I think.

BERNARDINO: Excellency, you realize, that although no one will be too upset if Çesare Borgia is cut down, to imprison his Holiness—well, that is something that has never been done. Spain will be compelled to join France against Milan—that would make for a very powerful alliance against Your Excellency.

LUDOVICO: Neither France nor Spain would dare attack Milan while Alexander is rotting in a dungeon! And not until we have his Holiness's word—signed and sealed—that he will disavow Louis' claim to Milan—not until then will he be freed! *(Pause)* I know what he has in mind, it is all too transparent. The Pope intends to legitimatize Louis' claim to Milan in exchange for the king's help in the Romagna. It is all part of a conspiracy to place the country under papal authority.

Blackout.

Scene x

Same time. A tavern facing an alley .

Leonardo, *looking quite out of place, sits with the* **Turk**.

THE TURK: Oh, we've been here going on six years. I lives in the back. It ain't much but it is all I has. Ya figure, what's a unsightly crooked rat like me to do outside? Ya'll conclude, 'not much.' So, I opens my hearth and allows my intimates to share a little o' themselves. I gets a cut, supplies the spirits and it is a proper business all around. It is a service to the city, I tells ya. Some may wonder as to the lack of godliness in this here room but, I do not care what the priests spew out; without sin, without a little evil, the world would be finished. Without a little evil, the priests would have nothing to do. Ya needs a little evil to make things move. Think of it! Can ya imagine everyone a saint? I can't. Can ya imagine a world of perfect goodness? I rather not. What would ya do from morn till night? Live and be happy? But how would ya know ya're happy if there's not a poor unhappy soul to compare with? See my point? The truth is ya can't expect everyone to be a saint and you wouldn't want to, either. Ha, ha, ha! Now, while we're on the subject of a little sin, I have somethin' for ya. Ya look like a learned man. By yer conversation I can tell ya're a learned man. I have a magical solution made from a flower that grows high above the Indus.

LEONARDO: A poison?

THE TURK: Nah, no poison. It's an elixir that brings about fantastical visions and rids the body of pain.

LEONARDO: Really?

THE TURK: I try it meself twice each day. I will be honest with ya, a man in my condition needs strong medicine and this is not only medicine—for likes I says, it rids the pain— but soothes the soul and makes a pleasure of life. Who can argue with that? Why not try some while you wait for this part'cular face yer lookin' fer? It is going to make the passin' time more pleasant, believe me. Would ya like a swig? This is gratis, a sample. Judge for yerself. I know that if ya try it, ya'll want more. He, he, he!

The **Turk** *attend his other customers.*

WHORE: What I'd like to know is why someone of your kind comes in here to sit by yourself! I do not understand it, I do not. You know, I can sit with you, besides you, on you, below you—
LEONARDO: No, thank you.

The woman grabs **Leonardo's** *crotch.*

LEONARDO: Do you mind!?
WHORE: Mind? Nah. I think one should always do as one pleases but—somehow I think it just ain't right you to be alone.
LEONARDO: I'm looking for something and it has nothing to do with you. Understand?
WHORE: Well, maybe I can help you find what you're lookin' fer. *(Seductive)* I can show you things you never imagined in you wildest fancies. How abouts somethin' tender—delicate?
LEONARDO: I beg your pardon?
WHORE: I have two young ones, luscious little darlin's. Pale, soft and so willin' to make you happy. You'd love 'em, I know you would. And they're ingenious. They have this game they like to play—they prop you up in bed and as you watch, they slowly help each other to disrobe. First their flowery little shirts, leavin' their soft young chests ready for your affectionate caress. Then, they embrace, like sweet little sisters they are, kissin' each other as they are left in the flesh. But, now, comes the good part— Listen! *(Pause)* They mount you from all sides, with youthful, exciting and tender anticipation, one on the right and one on the left. They have so much life in them, dear me. I guess I was as lively when I was ten!
THE TURK: Loretta! Get away! Ya ain't what he's looking for!
WHORE: Oh! *(To* **Leonardo***)* You want a boy? Why didn't you say so! I got my own little man but, it is gonna cost you extra, not much, mind you, well, he's six. But you know he's better than the girls and he does it all alone, he does, bless his little heart.
LEONARDO: Good God, woman, are you trying to sell your children?

WHORE: Selling? Who said anything about selling? *(Pause)* What do you have in mind?

LEONARDO: This is outrageous!

WHORE: Why? They like earning their own! What's wrong with that?

LEONARDO: No, thank you!

WHORE: *(Pause)* You wouldn't be looking for a stiff? I personally— if you ask me—I think it is twisted but if that's what you want— somethin' stationary?

LEONARDO: You are disgusting!

He tosses a few coins on the table and exits, leaving the green vial behind. No sooner he steps outside to door, that he is grabbed from behind, a knife placed against his side.

LEONARDO: How—how dare you!

THE THIEF: Quiet, or I'll rip out your cock and stuff it down your throat!

LEONARDO: Take—take what I have!

Leonardo *surrenders his purse.*

The **Thief** *grabs it and steps back. SOUND: Steps and conversation of someone approaching. He darts nervous looks about.*

Exit **Thief**.

Long pause while **Leonardo** *regains his composure. Suddenly, he returns inside the tavern and to the* **Turk**, *who is all the way in the back of the room.*

SOUND: Patrons talking and laughing and other noise.

We cannot hear what **Leonardo's** *tells the* **Turk** *but we can tell he is excited by the wild gyrations of his arms.*

THE TURK: *(To everyone)* Too much! Keep it down, people! *(To himself)* I can't hear myself think!

THE TURK: *(Cont.)* Oh, sir, you are very lucky, yes, you are. I knows who yer talking about and I tell ya, he's dangerous. And it doesn't matter that I do what I can to dissuade his kind–my more predatory patrons–from assaulting the rest of the clientele. I do, of course I do! It's not good for business and attracts the law. But, they pay no mind!

LEONARDO: What's his name?

THE TURK: Oh, ya likes him, eh? *(Laughs)* Well, he ain't got a name, not any more than the rest of the lowlifes ya sees in here have names. He, he, he! It is likes no one's ever been baptized and everyone's a bastard, he, he, he! All I can tells ya is he's called Stiletto! And, oh—he's a sharp one! Ha, ha, ha!

Slow blackout.

Scene xi

Next day. The citadel; **Ludovico's** *study.*

LUDOVICO: Where's Cecilia?

BERNARDINO: She is leaving for the country to await your pleasure. That is what you wanted, yes?

LUDOVICO: You mean she has not left yet? Please, keep her from view! If Beatrice as much as—

BERNARDINO: I am looking for a suitable candidate, Excellency. She is, after all, very close to our hearts.

LUDOVICO: To our hearts, yes, very much to our hearts. *(Pause)* Don't be too particular. I didn't like what she did the other day. Beatrice could have walked in and found her alone with me!

BERNARDINO: I am well aware of the implications, Excellency.

LUDOVICO: No, I dare say you are not. You are a widow these— how long has it been since your wife died?

BERNARDINO: Five years, my lord.

LUDOVICO: Five years that you have not had to put up with the unpredictable temperament and unreasonable demands of a woman.

BERNARDINO: Oh but I did.

LUDOVICO: Then your wife died.

BERNARDINO: She did.

LUDOVICO: *(Pause)* What—what was that she died of?

BERNARDINO: *(Pause)* She ate something she should not have.

LUDOVICO: Ah, yes, I remember now. Sad, very sad. Terrible loss, really. She was a noble woman.

BERNARDINO: She was an overbearing, evil hag.

LUDOVICO: Was she? *(Pause)* Oh, look. There is Maestro Leonardo now! *(Pause)* What is he doing here?

BERNARDINO: He has spent much of the day assembling the tail of the horse, Excellency.

LUDOVICO: The what?

BERNARDINO: The tail of the plaster model he plans to show Excellency.

LUDOVICO: When?

BERNARDINO: *(Yawns)* When he puts it together—could be soon—could be next year. Difficult to tell, with that man.

LUDOVICO: Oh, look—they are rolling it out— *(Pause)* Dear God!

BERNARDINO: *(Matter-of-factly)* I told Your Excellency it was a big horse.

LUDOVICO: And—there is no rider on top!

BERNARDINO: I beg your pardon?

LUDOVICO: I mean that by the time Maestro Leonardo puts my father on the horse the monument will reach the moon. It is—

BERNARDINO: Absurd, is the word I think you are looking for, Your Excellency. The monument is exceptional only because it is a monstrosity, a fantastic abomination created by a fool concerned only with the glorification of his pride, not the House of Sforza and certainly not the welfare of the duchy. I, of course, have an innate dislike for giant horses.

LUDOVICO: How many giant horses have you known, Counselor?

BERNARDINO: Only one and I can assure you that the Trojans were not amused. Yes, throughout history giant horses have been a source of great misfortune. At worst, they stink of treason. At best, they reek of folly. Frankly, I would not care if an earthquake dislodged the head of the horse as long as it landed on Leonardo Da Vinci.

LUDOVICO: Leave earthquakes out of it, Counselor. They cost lives and money. *(Pause)* I can't bare to look. This—horse is giving me a headache. Call him.

BERNARDINO: The horse?

LUDOVICO: *(Pause)* I'm not in the mood for humor, Counselor! *(Pause)* Call Maestro Leonardo—now!

BERNARDINO: Maestro! *(Pause)* Up here—here! *(Pause)* Would you mind terribly putting down the tail of your fabulous horse? His Excellency would like a word with you!

LUDOVICO: *(To himself)* I would like more than a word, to be sure!

BERNARDINO: He's on his way. *(Pause)* In fact, I can hear him running up the stairs.

Enter **Leonardo**.

LUDOVICO: Maestro Leonardo! *(Pause)* How are you?

LEONARDO: Out of breath.

LUDOVICO: How is the painting?

BERNARDINO: *(Aside)* Out of wall.

LEONARDO: I am making progress, Your Excellency.

LUDOVICO: Good to hear that, right, Bernardino? *(To **Leonardo**)* The abbot and the prior are driving me mad. Oh, I forgot to tell you that the holy father, Pope Alexander will be visiting Milan next week. I would like it very much if we unveil the fresco in his presence. What do you say?

LEONARDO: Next—?

LUDOVICO: I know I can count on you to have everything ready. I have to tell you, Maestro that when Princess Beatrice returned from the Grazie she—

BERNARDINO: *(Pause)* Bubbled.

LUDOVICO: Yes, that's one way of putting it. The Princess bubbled with praise for the fresco. She can not stop talking about it. *(Pause)* Although she rarely stops talking, period. By the way, Maestro, about the ball— *(Pause)* I appreciate what you are doing for her. I know how busy you are. I mean, who needs to be wasting time embroidering a dress and taking up hems? But what can we do, eh? Women are confoundedly irresistible! You know what I mean!

BERNARDINO: *(Aside)* He has no clue.

LUDOVICO: Now, Maestro, let's talk about the horse. *(Pause)* That horse is—beyond praise! *(Pause)* But—I think we'll have to put it—

LEONARDO: Where?

LUDOVICO: *(Pause)* Well, it's that I'm—

BERNARDINO: Mystified.

LUDOVICO: Y—yes, excellent word. Mystified, yes. I am mystified because, well, Corte Vecchia is too small for the monument, you see and people—they will not be able to appreciate its full measure. In other words, the horse needs to be placed where it can be enjoyed from a distance.

LEONARDO: Where?

LUDOVICO: Constantinople. *(Laughs)* I'm joking! *(Pause)* Maestro, that is one big horse! I had no idea; I never imagined and could not in a million years!

LEONARDO: *(Pause)* Your Excellency, the size of the statue is determined by the might and glory of the House of Sforza.

A smirk and shake of the head from **Bernardino**, *as if to say, "I knew he would say that!"*

LUDOVICO: That is true, all true and I'm grateful for the time you have spent on the horse. Am I not, Bernardino?

BERNARDINO: Without a doubt, Excellency—grateful, yes, very.

LUDOVICO: But you know, Maestro, fate never fails to bless me with extremes. I have a huuuge horse and a liiiittle problem and the size of the horse makes my little problem bigger, much bigger. *(In French)* Mon petit problem—is the King of the Gauls. He is small, you see—this size. *(Pause)* But although Louis is a small king, he has very big plans for Milan.

LEONARDO: Begging your pardon, Excellency but I do not understand what the Sforza monument has to do with the King of France. I apologize for my ignorance.

LUDOVICO: How much bronze do you need for the horse?

LEONARDO: Fifty tons.

LUDOVICO: Fifty!!! *(Pause)* Bernardino, how many cannons can we build with fifty tons of bronze?

BERNARDINO: Two and a half cannons per ton, Excellency.

LUDOVICO: You like numbers, Maestro, figure it out. Fifty tons of bronze will get me enough artillery to protect the city, because that is the only thing that will keep the King of France out of this room. Do I have to say more? *(Shrugs)* No cannons, no duke; no duke, no Leonardo.

BERNARDINO: If I may, Your Excellency. Maybe Maestro Leonardo should cast the horse in something else.

LUDOVICO: A wonderful suggestion! Maestro?

BERNARDINO: Excellency, Maestro Leonardo is a brilliant crafts-man, an artistic genius, a master, a man who we are proud to have as our own, someone who honors Milan with his presence. Without a doubt, the equestrian statue, regardless what it is made of, will be placed among the wonders of the world, its beauty and grace to remain unmatched throughout history!

LEONARDO: But, Excellency—Your Excellency, I—I designed special ovens to cast the bronze!

BERNARDINO: Begging your pardon, Excellency but it seems to me that for a man of Maestro Leonardo's incomparable artistry and ingenuity, refitting those ovens should be a simple matter, wouldn't you say?

LEONARDO: No! Your Excellency, to cast the horse in another metal, requires an entirely different process. Am I to discard everything that has been done up to now? To sit down and design another horse—because that is what I would have to do—would take an incredible amount of time.

LUDOVICO: *(Dryly)* Time you have, bronze you do not.

LEONARDO: Your lordship, I've worked with great sacrifice—even without pay because my one and only goal is to serve the Moor.

LUDOVICO: What was that? Without pay? *(Pause)* How long has it been since you were given your salary, Maestro?

LEONARDO: Two months.

LUDOVICO: What! But that is terrible! Oh, this is awful. I—I don't know what to say. Why didn't you tell me? How can this be possible? Bernardino, the man has to eat, you know!

BERNARDINO: I am sure it has been a misunderstanding.

LUDOVICO: Your account will be settled at once! Bernardino, call for the treasurer!

Exit **Bernardino**.

LUDOVICO: You do have another option—with the horse, I mean. You could scale it down a bit, I know you can. After all, *who* is the most talented, the greatest artist in Italy, maybe of the universe?

Enter **Bernardino**.

BERNARDINO: Bramante but he's busy.

LUDOVICO: *(Pause)* I was talking about Maestro Leonardo, Counselor!

BERNARDINO: Begging your pardon, Excellency. *(Pause)* Maestro, follow me, if you please.

Ludovico *turns his back on the artist as he bows and exits with* **Bernardino**. *Slow blackout.*

Scene xii

That night. **Leonardo's** *apartments . He is sprawled in a chair, as he tries to play the lute and sing.*

LEONARDO: *(Sings)* He killed the horse.
Why not the wall?
Cannons and fire.
All they aspire.
All they aspire.

There is no bronze.
What about stone?
A horse of stone—
Will not inspire.
Will not inspire!

Will not—will not—

Drunk, **Leonardo** *falls asleep.*

Enter **Lorenzo, Antonio, Marco** *and* **Salai**.

LORENZO: It's past three in the morning! Wake him up.
SALAI: Not on your life.
ANTONIO: It doesn't matter whether he wakes up on the floor or in his bed. He's going to feel like shit anyway. Besides, we would have to drag him to his room and he weighs twice as much as any of us. I say, leave him be.
MARCO: You could pour cold water over his head.
LORENZO: What will that do, genius, except give him a cold?
SALAI: He hates cold baths.
MARCO: Not a bath, stupid. I mean, to wake him up!
ANTONIO: Why!?
LORENZO: Because!
ANTONIO: Because what?
LORENZO: Because it helps to stick your head in cold water to avoid getting sick after getting drunk.

ANTONIO: Said who?
LORENZO: Me.
ANTONIO: And when was the last time you got drunk?
SALAI: Maestro, wake up!
MARCO: Eat him. If that doesn't do it, nothing will. Ha, ha, ha!
SALAI: Vaffanculo!
ANTONIO: Get away!
LEONARDO: What—what time is it?
LORENZO: Late.
SALAI: Very late.
LEONARDO: *(Sings)* He killed the horse.
        Why not the wall?
        Cannons and fire.
        All they aspire.
        All they aspire.
LORENZO: Come along, Maestro.
LEONARDO: *(Sings)* There is no bronze.
        What about stone—?
MARCO: *(To **Salai**)* I hate sleeping with a drunk.
SALAI: *(To **Marco**)* No need to worry about that!
ANTONIO: Will you girls stop it! Give a hand here! He's heavy!
LEONARDO: *(Sings)* A horse of stone—
        Will not inspire.
        Will not inspire!
        A horse of stone—
EVERYBODY: Will not inspire—a horse of stone—will not inspire!

*Exit **Leonardo** and the boys. **Lights** dim slowly as their voices fade out.*

Scene xiii

Next morning. The refectory.

MARCO: What's there to do?

LORENZO: That's not for you to question.

MARCO: Not to question? While Salai stays home, sleeping—screwing his master.

ANTONIO: What good is he, anyway? *(Pause)* Who's for a game of cards?

LORENZO: Set them up.

MARCO: *(On the scaffold)* I'm taking a nap.

ANTONIO: Peter and John are staring at you.

With his back to the wall, **Marco** *gives his friends "the finger."*

LORENZO: He'll stay home, I'm sure.

ANTONIO: This is so boring! I mean—we could be here all day!

LORENZO: That's what you get paid for.

ANTONIO: Paid? Who's getting paid? Marco, are you getting paid? *(Pause)* Neither am I!

LORENZO: You're getting paid—in other ways. You're learning—

ANTONIO: Crap.

LORENZO: Just deal and shut up.

ANTONIO: Why don't we go to town?

LORENZO: Are you mad? Maestro Leonardo can show up any time.

ANTONIO: You just said he's not.

LORENZO: He can change his mind.

ANTONIO: I bet I can take off my clothes and stand in the middle of this room all day and no one would be the wiser.

LORENZO: *(Pause)* You wouldn't dare.

MARCO: Of course he wouldn't!

ANTONIO: How much? I forgot, you have no money!

LORENZO: Neither do you.

ANTONIO: But I'll win, so I don't care.

LORENZO: And you'll stand naked in the refectory?

ANTONIO: Yes.

MARCO: How long?

ANTONIO: Two hours.
MARCO: You're on!

Enter **Fra Marcelino**.

MARCELINO: I beg your pardon. I am Fra Marcelino. I am looking for Maethtro Leonardo. I wath thupposed to come latht week but fell ill. I apologith if I have dithturbed your peath.
LORENZO: *(Pause)* I am Maestro Leonardo. Come in, please. Stand in the light where I can see you.
MARCELINO: Well, I—
LORENZO: What are you looking at?
MARCELINO: You're so young.
LORENZO: Thank you. Now, speak. I have things to do.
MARCELINO: Fra Bandello athked me to come by. He thsaid you were looking for thomeone for the picture.
LORENZO: What picture?
MARCELINO: I don't know. The prior never thaid what picture.
ANTONIO: *(Pause)* Maestro, maybe Fra Bandello meant the fresco?
LORENZO: That makes sense since we have no other picture here, do we? *(Pause)* So you want to pose for me, is that it?
MARCELINO: Pothe? I—I don't know. What do you mean 'pothe'?
LORENZO: You want to model for the wall, yes?
MARCELINO: *(Humble)* I wath told by the prior to do your pleasure.
LORENZO: A chair! *(Pause)* Sit.
MARCELINO: Why?
LORENZO: Because it is going to take time.
MARCELINO: I don't mind standing.
LORENZO: You will get tired.
MARCELINO: I will not.
LORENZO: *(Pause)* Very well. *(Pause)* Mmmm—
MARCELINO: What?
LORENZO: You have a long nose.
MARCELINO: And?
LORENZO: A small chin.
MARCELINO: So?
LORENZO: A wide forehead.
MARCELINO: Which means?

LORENZO: You ask too many questions. *(Pause)* Oh, this is impossible! How can I hope to catch the right perspective when your nose and head are out of proportion? I've never seen anything like it in my life. Are you sure Fra Bandello told you to come to me?

MARCELINO: Y—yeth he did. *(Pause)* What ith perthpective?

LORENZO: Perspective? Perspective—is everything!

ANTONIO: Not everything, Maestro.

LORENZO: Of course it is everything!

ANTONIO: Light, shadow and color are just as important as perspective.

LORENZO: Really? Says who?

ANTONIO: *(Smiles)* Says, you—Maestro.

LORENZO: *(Pause)* Ah, yes. The—boy is correct. Perspective is not everything.

MARCO: But it is very important.

Lorenzo *gives* **Marcelino** *a bucket.*

LORENZO: Put it on your head. *(Pause)* What are you doing!?

MARCELINO: *(Head in the bucket)* You said—

LORENZO: On top! *(From the scaffold)* Look here!

MARCELINO: What—what are you doing?

LORENZO: Finding the right angle.

MARCELINO: Oh.

MARCO: Which is different than perspective.

LORENZO: *(Pause)* There—there is something about you that I just do not like.

MARCO: Maestro, the bucket and the habit do not match.

LORENZO: You're right. *(To* **Marcelino***)* Off with the habit!

MARCELINO: What!

LORENZO: I can not draw you in that sack, that's all there is to it! It is out of the question. Forget it! I will find someone else.

MARCELINO: But, Methsser!

LORENZO: Go! Stop wasting my time!

ANTONIO: Maybe the shoulders, Maestro. After all, you need the face—

MARCELINO: I'll catch a cold!

LORENZO: No, you won't. This room is an oven!

Marcelino *drops his habit to his shoulders.*

LORENZO: *(Pause)* Oh, what a frightful sight! You insult my eyes! Cover yourself! *(Pause)* Are you French?
MARCELINO: French? Heavens, no!
LORENZO: Not Italian.
MARCELINO: Spaniard.
LORENZO: Figures—
MARCELINO: Maestro, how long doesth it take you to paint thsomething like that wall?
LORENZO: Months.
MARCO: Years.
ANTONIO: And it is still not finished.
MARCELINO: Why so long?
LORENZO: *(Imitating* **Leonardo***)* Well, it is more, much more than a painting on a wall. I am trying to represent the everlasting clash between Good and Evil. Let me show you. *(Pause)* Everything converges on the face of Jesus. It accentuates his solitude; He is alone even among his apostles. Don't you think that Christ's dignity, his aloofness and perfect calm sets him apart from the rest? Look! Christ extends his arms outward to the center of the fresco, his left hand reaching for a loaf of bread! Why, we witness as the Christ declares, 'This is my body which is given you; this cup is the new testament in my blood, which is shed for you.' *(Pause)* The apostles themselves are in groups of three—one, two—three and four. *(Pause)* On Christ's left, the Doubting Thomas, with his upward pointing finger. Here we have Bartholomew, guileless, his hands held to his breast. The one seated next to Jesus with arms outstretched, is James the Greater. On the far left, James the Lesser and Andrew. Notice—notice that Andrew sits beside his brother, Peter. And here, opposite them, Matthew, Thaddeus and Simon. *(Pause)* Two great arcs, one on each side connect the groups to each other! But, more important, they represent two dramatic poles, good against evil, one on the right and one on the left. On the left—left of Jesus, that is—faith and purity personified by Philip, who followed Jesus from the beginning! I've rewarded him by placing him above everyone else.

LORENZO: *(Cont.)* As you can see I've caught the instant when the Christ reveals, 'Amongst you there is one who will betray me!' The apostles emphatically display their torment! Their bodies recoil in dismay. They wonder who Jesus is talking about!

MARCELINO: *(Yells)* Judas!

LORENZO: Yes, Judas! That paragon of evil! That—bad man! *(Points)* There, he is! I've placed him lower than everyone else! Can you see there is an invisible straight line running exactly through the face of Christ connecting Philip and the Judas? Judas on the right of our Savior; Judas and the Christ, reaching for the same bowl. Overcome by shame Judas shrinks away because when their hands touch, Judas will be identified as the betrayer!

MARCELINO: I do! I see the line! Oh, Maestro, it isth magnifithcent!

LORENZO: It is all here, drama, ritual, betrayal, sacrifice and salvation! But, I haven't found the Good and I haven't found the Evil. That is where you come in.

MARCELINO: *(Pause)* Me? Isth that why you want to paint me? You want me to be the Chrith? You—you cannot do that!

LORENZO: Why not?

MARCELINO: I—I am but an insignificant, thordid fellow! How could I ever hope to—

LORENZO: Take it easy, friend. There is nothing to be ashamed of. *(Points to Marco)* I did his mother as—

MARCELINO: Thsacrilege! The saintly countenance of our lord Jesus Christ will be defiled by my unstheemly face! Pleaseth, don't! Pleaseth!

Exit **Marcelino**.

LORENZO: Wait! Come back!

ANTONIO: *(Laughs)* You did *his* mother!

MARCO: *(Laughs)* And *your* sister, whoreson!

LORENZO: Didn't look like Christ to me—

ANTONIO: *(Laughs)* —but a perfect Madonna!

Marco *runs up the scaffold and stands imitating* **Lorenzo** *imitating* **Maestro Leonardo,** *with a few added gyrations of the hips.*

MARCO: It is all here, drama, ritual, betrayal, sacrifice and salvation!

ANTONIO: I thought he was going to faint!

MARCO: Wait 'til Maestro Leonardo hears you've been making fun of him!

LORENZO: *(Serious)* And who's going to tell him?

MARCO: That little butterfly! He'll tell Bandello who'll tell Maestro!

LORENZO: *(Softly)* Maybe. And maybe I'll tell Salai you jerk off calling out his name!

MARCO: What!?

ANTONIO: Will you two shut up! If Fra Bandello—

Marco *throws a brush at* **Lorenzo**. *It lands on* **Antonio**.

ANTONIO: Porca puttana! My mother made this for me!

Antonio *returns fire and hits the fresco. Long pause.*

LORENZO: *(Pulling his hair)* Blessed Virgin Mother of God! Oh, my God!!!

Horrified, **Marco** *tries to get down from the platform but his jerkin gets caught on the railing. It pulls the structure out of place and sends everything crashing to the ground. Long pause.*

LORENZO: Oh shit.

Blackout.

End Act I

Second Act

Scene i

Same time. **Leonardo's** *apartments; his bedchamber.* *SOUND: Rain and thunder.*

LEONARDO: *(Groggy)* What are you doing?

SALAI: *(Half asleep)* Making sure you didn't fall off.

LEONARDO: What—time is it?

SALAI: Don't know. I think its mid-day.

LEONARDO: I have to get— *(Holds his head)* Ohhh!

SALAI: Stay in bed.

LEONARDO: *(Pause)* Where's—?

SALAI: They left early, said they were going to the Grazie. *(Pause)* I think Sofia's downstairs.

LEONARDO: *(Pause)* Do you know, that—shepherds in the Romagna at the foot of the Apennines, make peculiar large cavities in the mountains in the form of a horn and this horn becomes one and the same with the cavity and thus they produce a very loud noise by blowing into it?

SALAI: What?

LEONARDO: And did you know that there is a spring in Sicily which at certain times of the year throws out chestnut leaves in great quantities?

SALAI: Maestro—

LEONARDO: And—and that is quite strange, you see, because chestnuts do not grow in Sicily, hence it is evident that the spring must issue from some abyss in Italy and then flows beneath the sea to break forth in Sicily.

SALAI: What are you talking about?

LEONARDO: *(Pause)* I don't know. What did I say? *(In pain)* Oh! *(Pause)* Come here—

SALAI: No. My work is done. I kept you from falling off the bed— hurting yourself. Now I am resting. Servants have a right to rest.

LEONARDO: Stop it! Stop—this nonsense!

SALAI: Nonsense? Is it nonsense that you think of me your servant, that you do not love me?

LEONARDO: Of course I love you! How can I not love you? It is impossible for me not to love you! What is the matter with you!?

SALAI: So why didn't you answer me the other night? Are you ashamed? Why did you write to Messer Lucca that I was your servant?

LEONARDO: Salai! *(Pause)* I'm not feeling well.

SALAI: But, do you love me?

LEONARDO: *(Pause)* More than I can tell you.

SALAI: Try!

LEONARDO: How can—how can I make you understand how difficult it is for me. There are things—feelings I am forced to keep to myself. *(Pause)* There are—appearances to keep— *(Pause)* I—don't like feeling this way—Ohhhh!

SALAI: Don't drink. *(Pause)* Maestro—

LEONARDO: Uh?

SALAI: Who was your first lover?

LEONARDO: Oh, please! I'm not a well man!

SALAI: How old were you?

LEONARDO: I don't know—it was a long, long, long time ago.

SALAI: You don't remember your first lover?

LEONARDO: *(Pause)* My uncle.

SALAI: Did you love your uncle?

LEONARDO: Very much. *(Pause)* He was my best friend.

SALAI: And your second lover?

LEONARDO: *(Sighs)* My teacher.

SALAI: *(Laughs)* Maestro Verrocchio?

LEONARDO: Yes. You find that amusing?

SALAI: It is just that—

LEONARDO: He could not keep his hands off of me. Ohhh, my head.

SALAI: Did you love him?

LEONARDO: I liked him very much but I did not love him.

SALAI: Did he love you?

LEONARDO: He must have. He was always drawing me. Artists have a tendency to fall in love with their creation.

SALAI: Is that why you are always making pictures of me? *(Pause)* You reek of wine.

LEONARDO: You don't smell too good yourself.

Salai *cuddles up to Leonardo as the* **Lights** *dim slowly and go to black.*

SALAI: You do love me, don't you?

Scene ii

Later. The citadel; **Ludovico's** *bedchamber.*

SOUND: Rain and thunder

BEATRICE: Two days!

LUDOVICO: He has things to do, my darling. But, there is nothing to worry about.

BEATRICE: It's your fault. He told me!

LUDOVICO: My fault!

BEATRICE: Yes! You keep him so busy he has no time for anything else—including me!

LUDOVICO: I have time for you.

BEATRICE: Please stop that! You obviously think this is funny! My unhappiness amuses you, is that it?

LUDOVICO: Not at all, my darling. Far from it.

BEATRICE: So tell me! What if Maestro Leonardo—

LUDOVICO: If! What if an earthquake strikes and we are all swallowed by the earth? Many are the *ifs*, Beatrice! Maestro Leonardo will do what you ask and he will do it in time for the ball. Trust me!

Ludovico *tries, again, to make love to* **Beatrice**.

BEATRICE: No, I said!

LUDOVICO: Why not?

BEATRICE: I don't feel like it.

LUDOVICO: My darling—

BEATRICE: What?

LUDOVICO: Why are you being so—so difficult?

BEATRICE: Oh, I'm difficult, am I? I really do not understand you, Ludovico. First, you have all but said—in fact, I'm sure you said it in so many words—that you are not worried about Maestro Leonardo, knowing how important the ball is to me! If that were not outrage enough, I also find out that your whore—that cow, that witch's flint—is still at the palace.

LUDOVICO: She is not!

BEATRICE: Don't treat me like a child. Bernardino da Corte has made it his business to undermine my authority. He knows Cecilia Gallerani's presence at the palace offends my dignity, my virtue and that of my family! He knows it too well. Yet, he does what he likes!

LUDOVICO: *(Patiently)* Cecilia Gallerani left Milan—as you ordered.

BEATRICE: She did not! She's still here and under the protection of that horrible man!

LUDOVICO: You have been misinformed. Now, please, talk of something else.

BEATRICE: Do you know what I find incredible? That the Duke of Milan does not know when his chief of security is lying to him! Now, you might be willing to put up with it but I will not! I despise him. He's nothing but a pimp!

LUDOVICO: It is thanks to Bernardino that I have been able to keep my enemies out of Milan. *(Pause)* Beatrice—my love—

BEATRICE: Leave me alone. I'm trying to sleep!

Long pause. **Ludovico** *leaves the bed wrapped in a blanket, walks to the wall in the back of the room, turns and looks at* **Beatrice** *one last time, sighs, shrugs, pushes a secret compartment and disappears into the wall, as the room goes to black.*

Scene iii

Next morning. The refectory .

LEONARDO: What happened here? Lorenzo—

LORENZO: M—Maestro?

LEONARDO: Why did you re-draw the fish?

LORENZO: *(Pause)* Who said I— *(Pause)* I had to, sir.

LEONARDO: Why?

LORENZO: *(Pause)* I—well, I did not like the way it looked.

LEONARDO: I painted the fish myself. You think *your* fish is better than *my* fish?

LORENZO: Oh, no, no, no, sir, of course—of course not, Maestro, that is impossible, out of the question!

LEONARDO: Then, why did you redo the fish?

LORENZO: Well, you see, Ma—ma—Maestro Leonardo—

ANTONIO: It was an accident!

MARCO: Yes, it was! It was not on purpose!

LORENZO: *(On his knees)* I had to, Maestro! The fish was ruined!

LEONARDO: *(Calmly)* Oh? You don't say? *(Pause)* What happened? *(Pause)* Wait. Let me guess. *(Pause)* You became bored. Because you were bored, you engaged in some shameless pursuit—I don't even want to think what you were doing—when one of you— Marco—yes, it was you—he got up on the scaffold and threw something—a rag—no, no, a brush—you threw a brush at Antonio. *(Pause)* The brush hit Antonio— *(To **Antonio**)* —you were so angry, you returned fire, except that instead of hitting Marco, you hit the wall, the fresco and the fish. *(Pause)* Marco— who was on the scaffold—panicked. He tried to run down the scaffolding, got his jerkin caught on the railing, pulled the planks out of joint and brought everything down.

ANTONIO: I did not mean to hit the fresco, I swear on the Madonna! It was an accident!

LEONARDO: Of course you did not mean to hit the wall. But don't tell me it was an accident because it was not. *(Pause)* I don't believe for a moment you did it on purpose but that's beside the point, isn't it? What I mean is that it would not make sense for you to willingly destroy something you've worked on for so long.

LEONARDO: *(Cont.)* But, I ask, what were you doing throwing things at each other, eh? It was reckless, it was childish and showed a terrible lack of di-li-gence.

MARCO: In truth, Maestro—

LEONARDO: Pray, tell me the truth.

MARCO: I didn't throw the brush at Antonio. I aimed at Lorenzo.

LEONARDO: Then, you're a terrible shot, because you hit Antonio.

MARCO: Who told you?

LEONARDO: No one. First, when you arrived home last night, I noticed Antonio's shirt was stained—here. *(To **Marco**)* Then, your jerkin is torn. *(Pause)* The moment I walked in I noticed the scaffold had been moved and its legs reinforced, a clue that the structure collapsed and was put together again.

LORENZO: How—

LEONARDO: Look, for three years I have been going up and down that ladder, dozens of times each day. Don't you think I would notice even the slightest change in its position?

LORENZO: And the fish?

LEONARDO: Ah, well, the fish is good but it will be a sorry day if I can not tell the difference in styles, the difference between the master and the student. It is all observation, deduction and logic.

MARCO: Are you angry?

LEONARDO: Do I look angry?

ANTONIO: N—no.

LEONARDO: Should I be?

MARCO: Oh, no, no, please, Maestro, no!

LEONARDO: You did repair the fresco, fixed the scaffold and cleaned up. *(Pause)* Salai, you were lucky you weren't around!

SALAI: *(Laughs)* I know! They would have blamed me!

LEONARDO: Now, I want to try and finish this—this wall.

LORENZO: We're out of yellow, Maestro. Messer Lucca never sent it.

LEONARDO: Salai—go, find out what happened—bring back two bags and help Lorenzo. We will be at the citadel— *(Somewhat disgusted)* —dressing the princess for the ball! *(Calls after the boy)* No candy!

Exit **Salai**.

LEONARDO: *(To* **Antonio***)* Let's go.

Exit **Antonio** *and* **Marco**.

LEONARDO: *(To* **Lorenzo***)* And you, sir, since the fish needs no yellow, do it again.
LORENZO: The fish?
LEONARDO: Again.
LORENZO: Why? I thought you said it was—
LEONARDO: My dearest, the fish is good but it is not good enough for me.

Exit **Leonardo**.

LORENZO: Not good enough—not good enough—

Slow blackout.

Scene iv

Stage Left: *Street in front of* **Tomassino's** *shop.* **Salai** *enters.*

TOMASSINO: Psst!

SALAI: What are you doing?

TOMASSINO: I'm going crazy! Word's got out that Beatrice gets her candy from me!

SALAI: That's good, yes?

TOMASSINO: In a way, sure. But I can't leave the shop, not even for a few minutes. I'm up at four—I don't have time for anything anymore. It's bake and sell, bake and sell! You think you can get away and—

SALAI: Where to, now?

TOMASSINO: Same place. I'll give you twice the candy and a little change.

SALAI: *(Ponders-smiles)* Sure. I can always come back for pigment!

TOMASSINO: That's a good boy!

Lights *dim on the street.*

Stage Right: *The citadel:* **Beatrice's** *chamber.*

Enter **Leonardo**, **Antonio** *and* **Marco**. *The boys carry the costumes.*

LUDOVICO: Maestro Leonardo!

BEATRICE: Oh, Maestro! I'm so happy to see you. I thought you had forgotten about me!

LEONARDO: That, my dear lady, is impossible. I—just felt a bit under the weather—

BEATRICE: Oh, I know exactly how you feel! It *is* ghastly weather, Maestro, simply ghastly. Isn't there something you can do?

LUDOVICO: *(Laughing)* Yes, everybody talks about the weather. Only the great Leonardo will do something about it! What are you hauling today, Maestro? *(Laughs)* Not part of the horse, I hope?

LEONARDO: No, Excellency. These are the costumes for the ball I promised her ladyship.

BEATRICE: How wonderful of you!

LEONARDO: This is the outfit I mentioned, my lady. It resembles a rose—well, something like that beautiful flower—with a wide skirt made of thousands of petals that will be attached the afternoon of the event—to allow their natural fragrance to delight and marvel. *(Pause)* In addition to the gown, there is a magnificent hat of papier-mâché that depicts the blossoming flower in spring. It is a large hat—

LUDOVICO: *(Chuckle)* After all, it was designed by Maestro Leonardo!

LEONARDO: It is very light.

BEATRICE: And the Duke, Maestro? What is my husband going to wear?

Leonardo *pulls out another suit.*

LUDOVICO: Never!

BEATRICE: *(Pouting)* Oh but why?

LUDOVICO: Why? That is ridiculous, that's why!

BEATRICE: But, Ludovico! We will have so much fun! People will love it, you will love it, my darling, I know you will.

LUDOVICO: No!

BEATRICE: Please. I'll be—I'll be very—

LUDOVICO: Was this your idea, Maestro?

BEATRICE: It was my idea.

LUDOVICO: I know you want to dress in something special but why should I be sacrificed?

BEATRICE: Don't be cross.

LUDOVICO: *(Pause)* I'm not cross. How can I be cross with you? *(Laughs)* Let me see that buzz-ball!

Lights *dim on* **Stage Left**. *Action continues in* **mime**.

Stage Right: Bernardino's *study* .

Enter **Salai**.

BERNARDINO: Well, look who's here! What, more candy? Princess Beatrice certainly has a sweet tooth, doesn't she?

Bernardino *beckons the boy closer. He takes the box from the boy, places it on the table, reaches out and pulls* **Salai** *next to him.*

BERNARDINO: Giacomo, is it? *(Fondling the boy.)* Do you—do you know who I am?
SALAI: You are—his Excellency.
BERNARDINO: Oh, you *are* precious! *(Pause)* I am someone who can give you anything you want. Turn around. Mmmm. Tell me, Giacomino—do you like money?

Salai *hesitates before he allows for a timid nod.* **Bernardino** *sticks his hand inside the boy's shirt, then inside his hose.*

BERNARDINO: Are you getting, excited, Giacomo?
SALAI: S—sir!
BERNARDINO: Yes, my lovely?
SALAI: No, please sir, no!
BERNARDINO: Why not?

Bernardino *tries to undress* **Salai.**

SALAI: No!

Fearing for his life, **Salai** *shoves* **Bernardino.**

Stage Left: *Exit* **Leonardo, Antonio** *and* **Marco. Ludovico** *kisses his young bride.*

Exit **Ludovico. Beatrice** *tries the costume in front of the mirror.*

Stage Right: **Salai** *scrambles and picks himself up.* **Bernardino** *grabs him by the hair and throws him on the floor. The boy grabs a candlestick nearby and hits* **Bernardino** *across the head. The counselor reels back, holding his head in pain, giving the boy time to get away.*

Exit **Salai.**

BERNARDINO: *(Screams)* Murder! Murder! Guards! After him! He tried to murder me!

SOUND: Cries of "Murder" and "Stop! Murderer!" in addition to the sounds of clanging armor, are heard in the background.

Stage Left: *Enter* **Salai**.

BEATRICE: *(Calm)* Who are you?

SALAI: Oh, my lady! I—I came to deliver—to deliver candy and—and this terrible man tried to rape me! Please, save me, they're after me!

BEATRICE: Rape you! Who? What are you talking about? *(Pause)* Haven't I seen you before?

SOUND: Banging on the door.

SOLDIER: *(Off)* My lady? Are you in there?

SALAI: *(Crying)* Oh! Save me dear lady! They'll kill me! Save me!

Beatrice *points to the divan.*

BEATRICE: Hide, quick!

SOLDIER: *(Off)* My lady!?

Salai *hides.* **Beatrice** *throws the wide, voluptuous dress over the divan. Pause.* **Beatrice** *unbolts the door.*

Enter **Soldiers**, *followed by* **Bernardino** *and* **Ludovico**.

LUDOVICO: Beatrice!

BEATRICE: *(Angry)* What is the meaning of this?

LUDOVICO: There is an intruder in the fortress, a fiend who tried to murder Bernardino, then escaped into the hall.

BERNARDINO: He's dangerous and desperate, my lady!

BEATRICE: There is no one here but me. Post a guard outside if you want, now, please get out. I'm trying on my costume.

LUDOVICO: Tino! You and Fugazzi—guard the door! *(Yells)* And the rest of you, find him and bring him to me! *(To **Beatrice**)* Where's Silveria?

BEATRICE: Went for a needle and thread. *(Pause-softly)* There is nothing to worry about, Ludovico. You should be trying out your costume. Now, run along!

Exit **Ludovico**. **Beatrice** *bolts the door.*

BEATRICE: You can come out now. *(Pause)* You don't look like a fiend—No, don't cry. I'll get you out of here. What is your name?

SALAI: *(Sobs)* Giacomo.

BEATRICE: You *are* beautiful.

Beatrice *has sex with* **Salai**, *pulling him towards her and kissing him, first on the cheek, then on the lips, then on the neck, then on the other side of the neck. Before the boy knows what is happening,* **Beatrice** *has ripped off his shirt and is licking his nipples, first the one on the left, then the one on the right. Before* **Salai** *realizes what is happening,* **Beatrice** *pulls down his hose and has pulled him on top of her; before it dawns on* **Salai** *what is going on,* **Beatrice** *lifts up her skirt and he is mounting her.*

BEATRICE: *(Ecstasy)* Oh, oh!!!

Beatrice *is in a frenzy of passion; her legs wide open and she clutches at the boy. Pause.* **Soldiers** *break down the door.*

Enter **Soldiers**, **Ludovico** *and* **Bernardino**. *Pause.* **Ludovico** *stares at* **Salai** *on top of his wife.*

Salai, *tries to get away but* **Beatrice** *will not let go.*

BEATRICE: Rape! Ludovico! I have been raped me! Help me! *(To* **Bernardino***)* You! Is this what you call security! To be assaulted in my rooms!!!

LUDOVICO: Kill him!

BERNARDINO: Wait!

LUDOVICO: *(Screams)* Kill him I said!!!

Bernardino *grabs the* **Soldier's** *arm to stop him from killing* **Salai**.

BERNARDINO: Excellency, I need a moment with this wretch. We must find out who sent him and why! We must find out if he's part of a conspiracy! Sire, please, let me handle this!
LUDOVICO: *(Softly-enraged)* You know what to do.

Exit **Soldiers**, **Bernardino** *and* **Salai**. **Lights** *dim on* **Stage Left**.

Stage Right: Bernardino's *study. Enter* **Soldiers**, **Bernardino** *and* **Salai**.

BERNARDINO: Tie his hands behind his back and wait outside.

Exit the **Soldiers**.

BERNARDINO: You have made a terrible mess of things, Giacomo.
SALAI: Please, I beg you, don't hurt me, please, please!
BERNARDINO: Hurt you? I'm not going to hurt you, Giacomo. I leave the hurting to the experts. Too bad you have made the Moor angry. That was not very bright of you. Tell me—Beatrice wanted it, yes? You tried to hide in her room and she climbed all over you, right? Is that what happened? I don't blame her. *(Pause)* Oh, come now, aren't you going to rise for the occasion?

Bernardino *slaps the boy, then rapes* **Salai**. *The boy screams.*

BERNARDINO: I must say, Giacomo, you were certainly worth the trouble.

Blackout.

Scene v

Hours later. The refectory .

LEONARDO: *(Screams)* Where is he! *(To* **Antonio***)* Go find that little— *(Pause)* Start with Lucca's. See if Salai picked up the yellow. If not, bring back two bags so we can get this over with. I only have a few more hours of daylight! I'll have wasted the whole day!

Exit **Antonio**.

Leonardo *shows* **Lorenzo** *and* **Marco** *the drawing.*

LEONARDO: Let's at least finish the Christ. Well?
LORENZO: Perfect.
MARCO: Real perfect!

SOUND: A choir of friars sing.

Lorenzo *applies plaster on the wall, followed by* **Leonardo** *drawing the face of* **Fra Valentino**.

LEONARDO: Valentino, the teacher; Valentino, the wise. *(Pause)* We are created by the love of the One whose vision illuminates our lives and shows us the way to eternal glory! The One—the Father and Son, fused in our hearts so that we can create. The Father, who made us in His image, who sent us His only begotten Son, that we shall not live in everlasting damnation; that glorious spirit who has graced me with a miracle. I have found my Christ!

Enter **Antonio** *with bags of pigment.*

ANTONIO: Maestro!
LEONARDO: What is it? Where's—
ANTONIO: He wasn't at Lucca's but the man next door— Tomassino—said he paid Salai to deliver a box of candy to the citadel.

LEONARDO: When?
ANTONIO: This morning.

> **Leonardo** *slowly climbs down the scaffold and takes off his apron.*

LORENZO: *(Pause)* What's wrong?
LEONARDO: *(Pause)* I—I don't know. Go home—

> **Leonardo** *looks concerned.* *Exit* **Leonardo**.

> *Blackout.*

Scene VI

Later. **Stage Right:** *The citadel;* **Bernardino's** *study . He is putting back pieces of candy into the box that had been delivered by Salai. Pause.*

Enter **Soldier.**

SOLDIER: Maestro Leonardo—

Exit Soldier. Pause.

BERNARDINO: *(to himself)* Oh, what does he want now?

Enter **Leonardo.**

LEONARDO: Your Excellency—
BERNARDINO: This is a little late in the day, even for you. What is it? You look—
LEONARDO: One of my apprentices—he left this morning to pick up supplies and has not returned. It seems that—and I don't know exactly what happened—but I was told he came here.
BERNARDINO: Here? What on earth for? Was he—was he looking for you?
LEONARDO: Came to deliver sweets.

Bernardino *opens his eyes slowly and very wide at the same time he raises his brows, tilts his head to one side and tightly presses his lips into the faintest trace of a smirk. Suddenly, the intense pleasure he had derived from raping the boy is intensified by the realization that the boy had "belonged" to* **Leonardo.** *The delight is such, that* **Bernardino** *is forced to close his eyes and catch his breath.*

BERNARDINO: *(Sarcastic)* It can't be! No! Maestro Leonardo, this boy you're talking about, is he blonde with blue eyes? Was he dressed in a white shirt, a brown jerkin and a rose-colored hose? Is his name Giacomo? Is that who you mean? Take a chair, Maestro. You look pale.
LEONARDO: W—where is he?

BERNARDINO: Well, this is most upsetting. You see, if we *are* talking about the same young man, then I'm afraid I have terrible news for you, Maestro. Something quite unsettling has happened. This Giacomo—he raped Princess Beatrice.

LEONARDO: Your Excellency, Giacomo is just a boy. There must be a mistake!

BERNARDINO: I was there—I was with the Duke when he found your precious Giacomo humping Beatrice. There is just no way to describe the look on the Moor's face! *(Laughs)* I can tell you, Maestro, *I'll* never forget it! *(Pause)* And—let me give you a word of advice, for your sake—if you treasure your hide, make sure Ludovico does not find out Giacomo was your boy. He might decide to hang you as well.

LEONARDO: Hang!

BERNARDINO: Yes, hang. Or—what do you think the Duke should do to someone that just ravaged—forcibly, as we are told—his young princess? What punishment would you recommend for Giacomo? Banishment? A public whipping? And pray she does not become pregnant. *(Pause)* In any case, the Moor has decided; tomorrow, exactly at midday, Giacomo is to be broken at the wheel, hanged and what is left, tossed in the river.

LEONARDO: No, no! I can't accept that! This is wrong! Please, Excellency, I am begging you!

BERNARDINO: Come, man, show a little backbone!

Stage Right *goes to black.*

Stage Left: Beatrice's *room* . **Ludovico** *comforts his bride.*

LUDOVICO: Love, I think we should cancel the ball. You are in no condition to—

BEATRICE: I will recover. *(Pause)* I want Bernardino da Corte out of here, Ludovico! He goes or I'll tell father!

LUDOVICO: It is not that simple, Beatrice.

BEATRICE: Why not?

LUDOVICO: *(Pause–impatient)* How about this! The King of France has allied himself to the Pope.

LUDOVICO: *(Cont.)* The Pope is on his way to Milan, to—according to his Holiness—mediate peace between Louis of France and myself. *(Furious)* What he really wants, however, is for France to invade Milan! His trip here is nothing but a ruse! Do you imagine, in your wildest dreams I can afford to get rid of my most trusted advisor, my chief of security and my confidant at a time like this? What is the matter with you! There will be changes, I promise but for now—I suggest you grow up!

Slow blackout.

Scene vii

Later. The citadel; A dungeon.

The **Executioners** *are hovering over a torture contraption called "The Rack." The walls are adorned with axes to chop, ropes to hang, knives to slice, hooks to flay, saws to cut; vises, spikes, forceps, pincers, needles and branding irons, each item neatly arranged and accessible.*

FRANCO: *(Turning the crank)* Did you finish reading Livy?
AUGUSTUS: *(Sharpening a knife)* No. I put it aside for the moment.

The prisoner screams.

AUGUSTUS: I am reading Satyricon.
FRANCO: In Latin?
AUGUSTUS: Of course. There is not a worthwhile translation anywhere.
FRANCO: *(Turns the crank)* I would love to read it when you're through.
AUGUSTUS: Certainly.

Enter **Leonardo**.

FRANCO: Careful with your step, Maestro! It is a treacherous descent, to be sure!
AUGUSTUS: Good afternoon, Maestro.
FRANCO: Yes, good afternoon, Maestro Leonardo.
LEONARDO: Where is the boy?
AUGUSTUS: The boy? *(Pause)* What boy?
FRANCO: You know—the boy!
AUGUSTUS: Oh, that boy! What, are you thinking of cutting him up? He's younger than most, yes, the exception, eh, not the rule. Oh, the anxious expectation to peek inside someone limber, with organs and tendons that are pliable and supple, eh? You must be tired of dissecting old farts and hags, yes? Ha, ha, ha! I'm sure you are. Well, this one will be a treat. *(Pause)* How are you feeling? You don't look well.

LEONARDO: *(Gasping for air)* Where is he?

FRANCO: He is inside but we have orders, he's to see no one. Sorry.

LEONARDO: That boy is one of my students!

AUGUSTUS: *(Pause)* Are you serious? Is he, really? Oh, dear. Someone's made a mistake. Did you hear that, Franco?

FRANCO: I heard, I heard! That is just plain bad luck! *(Pause)* But you know what it is, Maestro, the truth is and I hate to say this but we have very few good men joining the military these days. It is mainly these peasant brutes who love putting on a helmet so they can go around bashing people in the head. They do a terrible disservice to the Duke, I think. I am sure they never took time out to find out who they were dragging off to prison.

LEONARDO: Please, help me get him out!

FRANCO: *(Pause)* We can't do that.

LEONARDO: Why not!?

AUGUSTUS: Rules. We can't release anyone, dead or alive unless we have a signed order from the Moor.

LEONARDO: I'll buy his freedom, then! How much do you want?

AUGUSTUS: Maestro, you know we would love to help you out, really but we can't.

FRANCO: What would we tell the Duke?

LEONARDO: That he escaped!

AUGUSTUS: Escaped? Ha, ha, ha! No one's ever escaped from here. You think the Moor will believe that a scrawny thing like that kid got away from us? *(Pause)* And even if it was arranged, they'll hunt him down; then they'll hunt you down; then they'll hunt us down. It would be our heads on the block and frankly, I don't think that's what you want. Certainly not what I want.

FRANCO: I'll do this much for you, in consideration of our acquaintance and that we hold you in great esteem, Maestro—since it is so important to you, I'll make sure the lad does not suffer before he's hung. I'll be extra swift so he feels no pain, how's that?

LEONARDO: I don't want you to be swift! I want you to let him go! Let me take him home!

AUGUSTUS: No, no. We cannot do that. And really, I think you better go, Maestro. I wouldn't want you to get in trouble with the Moor.

LEONARDO: Listen to me! I have gold—lots of gold. It's all yours if you set the boy free!

AUGUSTUS: Maestro, please!

FRANCO: If you want, bring him a blanket.

AUGUSTUS: That is an excellent idea—there are times when people stay here for months and months and you know how cold it can get in this place—but that is all we can do for you. Now, please—

LEONARDO: *(Screams)* Salai!

FRANCO: Enough of that, Maestro, please. You're making it very hard for us. Come, come.

Leonardo *is helped up the stairs by* **Augustus**.

Exit **Leonardo**.

AUGUSTUS: What do you think of that?

FRANCO: I really don't know what to think. I've never seen Maestro Leonardo so upset.

AUGUSTUS: Do you blame him?

FRANCO: No, can't say I do. I think I would be just as rattled if it was my kid getting the long end of the noose. I just hope the Moor doesn't want us to do anything fancy, after all, I did give my word to Maestro Leonardo.

AUGUSTUS: Remember we work for the Moor, not for Maestro Leonardo.

Franco *and* **Augustus** *continue working. Pause.*

AUGUSTUS: What's the matter?

FRANCO: *(Pause)* I was thinking—

Enter **Bernardino**.

AUGUSTUS: *(To* **Franco***)* How do they expect us to get anything done?

BERNARDINO: Well?

FRANCO: Nothing else, Your Excellency, not a peep. So far, we found out his name is Clodilio and he was born in Pavia. No mention of Naples, or anything else that might be construed as Neapolitan in nature, aspect or politics.

BERNARDINO: He looks dead.

AUGUSTUS: I can assure you, Excellency, he's not.

FRANCO: Indeed, Your Excellency, he's not too alive but he is indeed, still among the living.

BERNARDINO: Splash water on his face.

AUGUSTUS: I beg your pardon, Your Excellency, that will only get him wet. It will also make the floor very slippery.

FRANCO: Yes, Your Excellency, it is not a good idea. I slipped once and broke my hip. Besides, it is unnecessary. We have other means at our disposal. If you please, Excellency—step to the side, that's it.

Augustus *smothers the prisoner with a rag. The fellow moans and gasps.*

BERNARDINO: You're going to kill him!

FRANCO: With all due respect, Your Excellency, in twenty years— since leaving the order, in fact—we have never killed anyone we did not want dead. Augustus is just forcing the prisoner to—come up for air, if you will.

AUGUSTUS: We do our best to please. Sometimes I marvel at our own ingenuity. As you can see, this fellow is not too stout. We have taken great care to be firm, thorough and yet, managed to keep the level of damage within reason, so as not to carry him off, you understand. Nevertheless, it is my opinion—and I think Franco will concur—that we are wasting our time. I have no doubt that if he knew something else, he would have yelled it to the seven winds right from the first prick.

FRANCO: Quite right. In other words, Your Excellency, this one here can't talk if he doesn't have anything to say and no amount of persuasion is going to make a difference.

AUGUSTUS: I should add, Excellency, that if we stop now, well, he'll use his new condition of cripple to crowd the streets as a beggar. If we don't, please remember that there is a fine line between extracting information and extricating life. Of course, you tell us what you want and we will do our duty.

FRANCO: Our duty.

BERNARDINO: As always, I expect you to do your best. *(Pause)* By the way, Maestro Leonardo—

AUGUSTUS: He was just here.

FRANCO: And very upset.

AUGUSTUS: Said that kid your men brought in, is one of his students.

BERNARDINO: Was. He *was* one of his students—and I hope you did not let him see the boy.

FRANCO: We follow orders, Your Excellency.

BERNARDINO: Good. Excellent. Good work. Carry on.

Exit **Bernardino**.

AUGUSTUS: You were saying—

FRANCO: *(Pause)* Well, it's just that, I was thinking of Maestro Leonardo—

*The **Lights** go down slowly, as the two men apply their trade and their voices are drowned by the screams from their prisoner.*

Scene viii

About the same time. The citadel; **Ludovico's** *study* .

LUDOVICO: Maestro Leonardo? *(Sighs)* Show him in, of course.

Enter **Leonardo**.

LUDOVICO: Maestro, dear me, you look awful! Please, sit down.
LEONARDO: Excellency, something terrible has happened!
LUDOVICO: I'm listening, Maestro. You must bear with me, since you are responsible for this silly costume.
LEONARDO: Please, Excellency, I beg you—one of my boys—one of my students was arrested and is to hang!
LUDOVICO: What was that? When? Who gave the order? One of your students, you say? *(Pause)* No. The only wretch to hang is a whoreson who sneaked in the citadel and— *(Pause)* Anyway, that's it, I have not ordered anyone else to die. *(Pause)* Is it possible to tighten the waistline a bit, Maestro? What do you think? It is too loose, I think. See what I mean?
LEONARDO: Your Excellency, I beg you! That—wretch, as you call him—his name is Giacomo Caproti. He is fourteen. He has been living in my house since he was ten years old and all I can say is that it has to be a mistake! Salai—I call him Salai—he gets in trouble like most children but he's a child! *(Pause)* I can't explain what happened, Excellency. Messer da Corte said Salai was found in—in the Princess' chamber! *(Pause)* How is that possible!? I told Messer da Corte that I sent Salai—
LUDOVICO: *(Pause)* Are you telling me that miserable pig who raped my wife is your catamite? Is that what you're saying?
LEONARDO: Excellency!
LUDOVICO: Silence!!! *(Pause)* He was fucking my wife! I saw him!
LEONARDO: *(On his knees)* My lord, something is wrong. Please, I beg you, find out what really happened! Hold me responsible, if you will. I'll—I'll make restitution—whatever—I'll work for nothing, do your bidding, just please, don't kill him—he's—he's like my own son!
LUDOVICO: Your son? Your son!!! Don't make me laugh, fool!

Ludovico *tears the costume to shreds.*

LUDOVICO: Oh, this is too precious for words! Who cares what I've done for Milan! Who cares that I transformed a rustic trading post into the financial, cultural and industrial center of Italy, into the most magnificent city in Italy, maybe in the world! Who cares!? From now on I will be known as the "horned Duke"— owe my claim to fame to the ill-advised misadventures of Maestro Leonardo's little bugger!

LEONARDO: Excellency, I beg you—reconsider! I—I am overcome with grief, not only for what has befallen Salai but for the pain and shame this unfortunate incident is causing you and your bride. And yet, how was it possible for a boy like Salai, a small, frail boy like him to get into the citadel when he was supposed to be somewhere else! Not only that, how was he able to get in the room with the princess? I beg you! Do not smother the life of a child while there is the slightest doubt of who is responsible! *(Pause)* Show the world you are a true faithful servant of Christ, willing to be impartial at a time when hatred blinds your sense of righteousness!

LUDOVICO: Oh, shut up! Shut up and get out! Get out before I forget myself! Guards!

LEONARDO: This is an outrage! You are murdering an innocent child!

Enter **Soldiers**. *The grab* **Leonardo**.

Exit **Leonardo** *and* **Soldiers**.

LUDOVICO: *(Pause)* Bernardino!

Enter **Bernardino**.

BERNARDINO: Your Excellency?
LUDOVICO: You forgot to mention that that whoreson who— raped Beatrice is one of Maestro Leonardo's—apprentices.

BERNARDINO: I learned about it only this morning. I judged the information irrelevant and decided that to tell you would have upset you further, distracting you and—given that the holy father is on his way to Milan and that the French are poised at the border, you really need to keep your wits about you, Excellency; the survival of the duchy is at stake. Everything else, including Leonardo da Vinci, is of little consequence.

LUDOVICO: What was the boy doing in your rooms?

BERNARDINO: Delivering candy.

LUDOVICO: *(Pause)* Why did he hit you over the head?

BERNARDINO: *(Matter-of-factly)* I guess he took offense that I grabbed his crotch.

LUDOVICO: *(Matter-of-factly)* And why did you do that?

BERNARDINO: It amused me.

LUDOVICO: *(Pause)* Your amusement has caused me a lot of grief, Counselor.

BERNARDINO: My apologies, Excellency. *(Pause)* I will only say that, had it not been for Princess Beatrice's ill-advised fraternization with the young man, he would have been arrested without incident.

LUDOVICO: *(Long pause)* Maestro Leonardo is no longer welcome in Milan.

BERNARDINO: *(Pause)* I take it, then, you have changed your mind about—the horse?

Ludovico *throws the statuette against the wall.*

LUDOVICO: There will be no horse—at least not one by Leonardo da Vinci! *(Pause)* Guard!

Enter **Soldiers**.

LUDOVICO: Bring Princess Beatrice to me, now! If, for any reason, she hesitates, drag her by the hair, if you have to!

BERNARDINO: Your Excellency—*(Pause)*—remember her father is the duke of Ferrara, your ally! You can't afford more enemies!

LUDOVICO: Get out!

Exit **Bernardino**.

Enter **Beatrice**.

BEATRICE: How dare you send for me like a commoner!

> **Ludovico** *slaps her, knocking her to the ground. He follows with kicks and a leather strap.*

LUDOVICO: Whore! You fucked him didn't you? What is it, you don't like men? You have to go and fuck a pansy, a little bugger— Leonardo da Vinci's lover! You monstrous bitch!

> **Ludovico** *rapes* **Beatrice**. *She screams.*

> *Long pause. A satiated* **Ludovico** *gets up from the floor.*

LUDOVICO: Bernardino!

> *Enter* **Bernardino**.

LUDOVICO: I want *Princess Whore* stripped and whipped!
BERNARDINO: *(Pause)* Yes, Excellency. Guard!

> *Enter* **Soldiers**.

BERNARDINO: Take her away—
LUDOVICO: And send for Cecilia!

> *Blackout.*

Scene ix

Later. The citadel. The dungeon .

Franco *sharpens a very long and thin blade, while* **Augustus** *removes* **Clodilio**, *the unfortunate, reputed spy from the rack.*

FRANCO: Ready?
AUGUSTUS: Yes.
FRANCO: No second thoughts?
AUGUSTUS: When have you seen me have second thoughts? I leave second thoughts to others.

Exit **Augustus**.

FRANCO: *(Calls out)* I am sorry I'll have to break my promise to Maestro Leonardo.

Enter **Augustus** *and* **Salai**.

The boy is terrified; stares at the monster holding the blade.

SALAI: No, please!

Slow blackout as **Salai** *screams.*

Scene x

Early that evening. **Leonardo's** *apartments .*

Enter **Leonardo** *and the boys.*

ANTONIO: Maestro, please, calm down!

Lorenzo *and* **Marco** *light candles.*

LEONARDO: Calm down! Don't you understand!? They're going to murder Salai!

Marco *walks up to* **Leonardo** *and puts his arms around his master.*

MARCO: *(Sobs)* Maestro, please!
LEONARDO: *(Aside)* 'Do you love me?' he said.
THE THIEF: *(Off)* I'm moved but I would rather be on my way.

Enter the **Thief**.

LEONARDO: W—what are you doing here?
THE THIEF: What am I doing here? We have a mutual friend. He said you wanted to meet me. That's what the Turk said and the Turk is an honest swine. Didn't you tell him where you lived? Here I am.

SOUND: **Sofia** *screams.*

THE THIEF: She didn't come to no harm. *(Pause)* So—what do you want me for? The Turk said it'd be worth it—at least that's what the Turk said and the Turk is a truthful porker. He, he, he!
LEONARDO: *(To* **Lorenzo***)* Make sure she's all right—and stay in your room. I need a few minutes alone with this man.

Exit the boys.

LEONARDO: *(Pause)* You don't remember me, do you?

THE THIEF: Can't say I do, don't care to, either. *(Pause)* It so happens I rarely meet someone twice.
LEONARDO: Please, stand by the candle.
THE THIEF: What for?
LEONARDO: *(Pause)* I—I need to see you in the light.
THE THIEF: I said, what for?
LEONARDO: What for?
THE THIEF: Are you deaf? What is it you want from me?

Enter **Sofia** *and the boys. She has a large carving knife in her hand. The* **Thief** *draws his knife.*

SOFIA: Maestro!
LEONARDO: Out!!!
SOFIA: Maestro! That man—that man—
LEONARDO: Lorenzo! Antonio, get her out of here!

The boys grab **Sofia** *and gently lead her outside.*

Exit **Sofia** *and the boys.*

LEONARDO: *(Pause)* You were saying?
THE THIEF: What was I to do? I knocked like a gentleman and she wouldn't let me in! I wasn't about to argue. *(Pause)* Now, what do you want me for?
LEONARDO: *(Pause)* I want to draw your likeness—if you can sit still for five minutes.
THE THIEF: *(Shrugs)* What's the catch?
LEONARDO: No catch. You will be paid seven soldi.
THE THIEF: Fourteen.
LEONARDO: As you say—

Leonardo *picks up his notebook and pencil.*

LEONARDO: The hat—take it off.

Quickly, **Leonardo** *draws the face. Enter the boys. They keep to the door.*

LEONARDO: Did anyone ever tell you that you smell like a rotting carcass? *(Pause)* Did anyone ever tell you that you are a loathsome, despicable man?

THE THIEF: Did anyone ever tell you, you have a big mouth?

LEONARDO: You are a leering, detestable scum. *(Pause)* I was right to think you could stand in for the Judas.

THE THIEF: Vaffanculo!

Leonardo *stares at the picture he drew and makes a couple of quick adjustments. Pause. The* **Thief** *put his hat on and his hand out.*

LEONARDO: I'm finished. Get out.

THE THIEF: Money.

LEONARDO: Fourteen soldi, yes? That is six soldi less than you took from me at knife point. But I forgot—you don't remember! *(Pause)* What are *we* to do? You'll think I've taken advantage of your good nature—making you come all the way out here and leaving you empty-handed!

THE THIEF: *(Softly)* I'll rip out your eyes.

LEONARDO: No, you will not. *(Pause)* You are out of your element, here. You are not in some fetid, dark alleyway but in a well-lit room, face to face with a man who is very, very— *(Screams)* — upset! Now—get out of my house!

Long pause. The **Thief** *frowns, confused.*

LEONARDO: ARE YOU DEAF!?

The boys look at each other, horrified that **Leonardo** *is about to be murdered. Pause. Suddenly, the* **Thief** *throws back his head and laughs as he tries to stab the artist.*

Deftly, **Leonardo** *steps to his left and with the agility of an expert fencer, strikes the* **Thief** *with powerful blow to the side of the head, knocking the thief to the ground. The* **Thief** *scrambles to get back on his feet.* **Leonardo** *kicks him in the ribs, forcing him to drop the knife. Then,* **Leonardo** *grabs the* **Thief** *by the throat, squeezing his windpipe.*

LEONARDO: Next time—I'll kill you! *(Calls)* Lorenzo, the window!

Lorenzo *opens the window.*

Exit the **Thief** *(by way of the window).*

The boys run to look out the window. Pause. Then, they return to **Leonardo**, *embracing him, as they all break into tears. Slow blackout.*

Scene xi

Same time. **Stage Left:** *The Vatican; the* **Pope's** *apartments. His Holiness is meeting with* **Çesare**.

Stage Right: *The citadel;* **Bernardino's** *study . He is not there. Another man, his back to the audience, can be seen standing in the shadows.*

THE POPE: We leave tonight. I like to travel at night.

ÇESARE: Everything is arranged.

THE POPE: What about this man—the one that was building great weapons for Ludovico?

ÇESARE: His name is Leonardo da Vinci and he is not building weapons. In fact, there *are* no weapons, only a few blueprints and model-toys that Maestro Leonardo has built based on his infinite imaginings.

The **Pope** *picks up a letter from the table.*

THE POPE: And this letter? *(Reads)* I shall endeavor, without prejudice to anyone else, to explain myself to Your Excellency showing Your Lordship my secrets— *(Stops reading)* —and on and on.

ÇESARE: Nonsense. It is, if I may add, the extravagant, arrogant and overconfident musings of a suspect virtuoso.

THE POPE: So, the letter is a forgery?

ÇESARE: No. The letter is real, Holiness. Maestro Leonardo told us himself about it. *(Pause)* He was trying to impress the Duke of Milan, to secure a position at court. *(Pause)* What is important, is not what it says in the letter but that we have an influential asset in the Milanese court.

Stage Right: *Enter* **Bernardino**.

Machiavelli *turns to face him, as* **Lights** *dim on* **Stage Left**.

BERNARDINO: I apologize for having you wait but the Moor held me back.

BERNARDINO: *(Cont.)* He wanted to make sure that I conveyed to Your Excellency his most heartfelt welcome to our city. *(Pause)* Is the Pope on schedule?

MACHIAVELLI: He is.

BERNARDINO: So, let us review, then. *(Pause)* First, I have ordered General di San Severino to reposition the ducal troops south of the city. That is where Ludovico will ride out to meet Alexander, whom he will escort—with a small contingent of bodyguards—inside the city-walls. *(Pause)* Once here, the papal procession will head for the monastery of Santa Maria delle Grazie, for the unveiling of Maestro Leonardo's Cenacolo. *(Pause)* In the meantime, the north gate will be opened. Çesare and three thousand troops, will enter and follow to the citadel which, by then, will have been abandoned by my men. With the citadel secured, the French troops will march in from the west and surround the ducal troops—I will offer di San Severino safe conduct out of Milan—it's either that, or hang. He is a practical man. *(Pause)* The Moor—well, I leave to you. Have I left anything out? *(Pause)* Good. Please—my most sincere apologies to his Holiness and to prince Borgia. Tell them I will hopefully meet them some other time, perhaps, when the political climate is not so stimulating.

MACHIAVELLI: Suffice to say that they are most grateful for your help. Payment for said gratitude will be delivered to your residence, once Milan is under our control and his Holiness has returned safely to the Holy See, of course.

BERNARDINO: I have always said that it is very important for men like us to understand historical currents and even more important to know when to step aside, so as not to be swept away or crushed by indifferent fate.

Pause. **Bernardino** *offers* **Machiavelli** *his obeisance.*

Exit **Machiavelli**.

Lights *dim* **Stage Right** *and come up* **Stage Left**.

ÇESARE: As I said, Leonardo da Vinci is painting walls for Ludovico, not building weapons.

THE POPE: So much the better. *(Pause)* Did I mention that Louis has asked that his marriage be annulled so he can wed Ann of Brittany?

ÇESARE: On what grounds?

THE POPE: That he was married by force when he was a youth.

ÇESARE: Rather impulsive of the king. Louis is not only taking the throne but marrying the widow of the late king. *(Pause)* And your answer?

THE POPE: One that will make Louis grateful and willing.

Blackout.

Scene xii

Same time. The refectory .

LEONARDO: Let's get this over with! Lorenzo, the notebook.
LORENZO: *(Looks at notebook)* He is ugly.
LEONARDO: Worse than that. He is evil.

> **Leonardo** *applies wet plaster to the wall, in the spot where the face of Judas is to be represented. Then, with the boys watching, the artist begins to put the finishing touches to the fresco.*

LEONARDO: Yes—I think this will be finished today.
ANTONIO: I'll believe it when I see it.
LEONARDO: It's been worse than a crusade.
LORENZO: You only took a year on the Adoration—
ANTONIO: And less than that on the Annunciation.
LEONARDO: They were not as intricate. I can tell you—I'll never do another wall.

Enter **Bandello**.

BANDELLO: Maestro! Did you hear the news? Did you hear the great, great news?
LEONARDO: No. *(Pause)* What news?
BANDELLO: The Pope arrives tomorrow and the Moor has invited him here to see your masterpiece. Oh, it is a great honor, Maestro, a great honor!
LEONARDO: I know.
BANDELLO: You do? Who told you?
LEONARDO: It's not important.
BANDELLO: Not important? How can you say that?
LEONARDO: I mean—
BANDELLO: I can tell you the abbot is beside himself—almost leaped from his sandals when he heard the news. We've never had a Pope visit us before. *(Pause)* Wait a minute. You're not finished! How can the Moor invite the Pope to an unveiling if the wall is not finished! Oh, this is a disaster! Doesn't the Moor know it is not finished!?

LEONARDO: It will be finished, brother.

BANDELLO: Praise heaven! *(Pause)* You found them, then?

LEONARDO: Found them?

BANDELLO: Your models for—

LEONARDO: Look for yourself. *(Points to the wall)* There is the Christ— *(Shows the notebook)* —and here is the Judas.

BANDELLO: Frightening!

LEONARDO: You have no idea.

BANDELLO: Oh, blessed be! It is a miracle! A miracle! *(Pause)* You don't know what this means! *(Pause)* What is the matter, Maestro, you don't seem too happy. I don't blame you. So many years working on something and one day, that's it—it belongs to the rest of the world, eh, Maestro? *(Pause)* I cannot say I am not grateful this episode of the wall is at an end, I cannot say that. And I'm sure you're glad as well, eh? He, he, he. I guess we will have to get used to the idea. We will have to get something else to do. Dear God! I'm so used to running back and forth, trying to keep up with you! But it will be better all around. I mean the brothers can come back and sit together for their meals, like before. *(Pause)* I'll tell you a secret, Maestro. Do you know why I used to get so exasperated when you were not working here?

LEONARDO: You mentioned it once or twice.

BANDELLO: Before you came to us, I thought painting and such, a waste of time, a frivolous pursuit commissioned by men with a peculiar sense of priorities. Why not spend the time and the wealth wasted on such endeavors doing God's work, I thought— like feeding the sick and poor? Then I watched how you and your students struggled with the wall, day after day, month after month, year in and year out. I saw that flat, white piece of nothing come alive! Ah, Maestro, it is you up there on the wall. On Simon, Thaddeus, Paul—the grace of your soul is inevitably stamped on the face of the Christ.

LEONARDO: Inevitably, on the face of the Judas.

BANDELLO: I consider myself very lucky to have seen you give life to that wall. *(Pause)* And you know, I'm going to miss you.

LEONARDO: *(Smiles sadly)* As much as I will miss you.

BANDELLO: Oh, I must go tell the abbot!

LEONARDO: Brother—I have allowed you to see the wall but no one else, not until it is unveiled tomorrow.

BANDELLO: I understand, Maestro. *(Pause)* Oh, blessed be! It's miracle!

Exit **Bandello**.

LEONARDO: Marco, shut the door. No more interruptions. I am not stopping until this wall is done!

Leonardo *mounts the scaffold as we slowly go to black.*

Scene xiii

Next morning. **Stage Right:** *The citadel;* **Ludovico's** *study .*

SOUND: Trumpet call. Pause.

Enter **Ludovico** *and* **Bernardino**. **Ludovico** *is dressed as befits one who is about to receive the* **Pope**.

LUDOVICO: Seal the citadel until my return. No one is to leave or enter the palace. We are now at war.

Enter **Beatrice**.

LUDOVICO: *(To* **Bernardino***)* Leave us.

Exit **Bernardino**.

LUDOVICO: *(Pause)* You are, once again, our mistress; you are, once again my wife. *(Pause)* Yet, what happened, happened and it cannot be forgotten. You will regain your privileges as befit your station but even though you have regained our favor, you have lost forever the moral imperative to demand anything from us. Therefore, I will pursue whatever entertainment I please and I will not tolerate jealousy, childish tantrums or any other display of ill-humor. If you do not think you want to continue in Milan, I will have you returned to your father. If not, think of becoming a mother, you need something to divert your many interests and children can be quite amusing. Go back to your rooms. I have to go and meet the Pope.

Beatrice *curtseys and exits.* **Ludovico** *looks after her.*

LUDOVICO: Maybe the secret to handling temperamental women is to throw them in a dungeon for a week or two. Live and learn!

Exit **Ludovico.**

Lights *dim* **Stage Right**.

Stage Left: Beatrice's *room* .

Enter **Beatrice**. *She sits at her dressing table. Long pause. She sobs, then angrily wipes off her tears. She sighs and takes a candy from the box on the dressing table.*

SOUND: Trumpets call. **Beatrice** *looks out the window. Enter* **Bernardino**.

BEATRICE: *(Startled)* How dare you come in here without being sent for! How dare you!? The Moor will hear of this!

BERNARDINO: I am afraid he will not.

BEATRICE: You impertinent wretch!

BERNARDINO: I may be impertinent and I may be a wretch. You, on the other hand, are a pitiful and misguided bitch without a trace of grace, charm or intelligence.

BEATRICE: *(Screams)* Get out! Guards!

BERNARDINO: There is no one outside. But soon, this place will be crawling with papal troops. *(Pause)* Oh, dear. You look rather pale. Are you feeling well? *(Pause)* Oh, I see, you have been enjoying the candy. *(Pause)* Delicious, yes? *(Pause)* My wife had a similar fondness for sweets. *(Pause)* Soon, very soon, you will be flat on a slab—it rhymes!—stiff and black, which rhymes with flat and slab! *(To himself)* Did I miss my call in life? *(To* **Beatrice***)* No matter. There is nothing you can do. Worms will feast on you the same way you have feasted on anise comfits. Personally, I think it is better this way. You will not live to witness the fall of Milan. Yes, Milan is taken and you are going to hell. Good day, ma'am. Your father, the duke of Ferrara, should have taught you to choose your enemies as carefully as he chose your husband.

Bernardino *fixes his bonnet, bows very low and exits.*

Beatrice *screams as we blackout.*

Scene xiv

Same time. The refectory . The place has been cleaned, a carpet laid on the floor, where a large, ornate chair has been placed for the **Pope**.

Enter the papal procession Including **Ludovico**, **Leonardo** *and the boys,* **Fra Bandello**, *the abbot, friars and a few princes of the church, including* **Ludovico's** *brother,* **Cardinal Sforza**.

The wall is now covered with embroidered silk and a gold rope, with a large tuft, waits to be pulled.

LUDOVICO: Holiness, Maestro Leonardo has labored on the fresco for three years. It is a work that celebrates not only the greatness of our Lord and Savior but the formidable determination of the human spirit! Milan is proud, dear Father, that you can witness the fruit and artistic legacy of the greatest artist of our times! This blessed event is hereby dedicated to the greatness of Rome and Peter's successor! *(Pause)* Maestro, when you are ready.

Leonardo *bows and walks to the wall. He is about to give the go-ahead to* **Lorenzo**, *when he stops and turns to the* **Pope**.

LEONARDO: Holiness, this wall you are about to see decorated by my limited grace has been a source of inspiration and joy. Only in the last couple of days was I able to bring together all the elements that would project everything I wanted to convey in the painting. When the curtain is pulled by my apprentice, you will see many things. As you race your eyes from side to side, you will discover—from the beatified features of Christ and the distorted treason of Judas—what I myself discovered when I finished working on the fresco. You will see reflected in the faces of Simon, Thaddeus, Bartholomew, in short, on the features of every apostle in the Cenacolo, the doubt, the horror, the sudden awareness that regardless of who we are, regardless how much power, money or fame we may have, if we are mortals, we are not masters of our destiny. *(Pause)* Perhaps, Holiness, as the descendant of Peter, you can tell me why?

LEONARDO: *(Cont.)* Why must we, we who are citizens of this mighty land, live in fear of men who murder children, men who crush heads, maim and torture in order to submit their fellow human beings to their abominable whims? Who are these men that control our lives? *(Pause)* Who are these men who order the flesh of innocent victims to be stripped and then break their bones to make them suffer in undescribable pain! *(Glaring at* **Ludovico***)* Who are these men! Who are these men that dare, against all the teachings of our heavenly father, to commit such atrocities! Who are these men? Who are these devout and learned fellows that spend mornings in solemn prayer, then, with sweeping mandates justify hanging a child? Who gives them that right? How dare they? Who are these men!?*(Pause)* What good is it to create splendid treasures for the world to enjoy, treasures to embellish our lives with charm and civility, when we are at the mercy of tyrants! It is pointless!

Ludovico whispers something quickly in the **Pope's** *ear and walks slowly to* **Leonardo**. *He lays his hand on the artist's shoulder.*

LUDOVICO: Thank you, Maestro for those illuminating words. *(Stern)* Now, show the painting!

Leonardo *nods to* **Lorenzo**. *Pause.*

Enter **Çesare** *and* **Machiavelli**.

Unlike the heavy, ugly tarp, the silk curtain floats gingerly and quietly until it settles gracefully on the ground to reveal the completed fresco. The painting is received with due reverence. After what may have seemed like a very short time, the **Pope** *leaves his chair, walks up to the wall and laughs.*

THE POPE: Maestro Leonardo, this painting has surpassed our expectations! *(Laughs)* Çesare! Where is Prince Borgia?

Çesare *steps forward, his handsome and proud bearing contrasting with the homeliness of those around him. He stands beside the* **Pope**.

THE POPE: This is amazing, Çesare. Did you know you were chosen for the Christ?

LEONARDO: What!?

LUDOVICO: What is that?

MACHIAVELLI: *(Aside to* **Leonardo***)* The man you called a conquering despot, the personification of evil.

LEONARDO: *(Turns to* **Çesare***)* Fra Valentino!?

THE POPE: Duke of Valentinois, Maestro. A titled conferred upon Prince Borgia by the King of France.

LEONARDO: No!!!

ÇESARE: I'm sorry you are disappointed, Maestro.

LUDOVICO: *(Screams)* You'll hang for this!

Immediately **Çesare** *positions himself between* **Leonardo** *and the* **Duke***. His bodyguards, disguised as friars, throw back their habits and display their weapons. They secure the room and disarm* **Ludovico***.*

ÇESARE: Excellency Ludovico Sforza, by the authority invested in me by his Holiness Alexander VI of Rome, as Commander of the papal army, let me advise you that Milan is now under my Protectorate. *(To his soldiers)* Take him away to wait for the King of France.

Exit **Ludovico** *and* **Cardinal Sforza***.*

THE POPE: Çesare, you will tell me how you got your face on that wall, won't you? *(Pause)* Maestro, we are in your debt! It is a wonderful achievement, this wall of yours. *(Pause)* Would you be interested in doing another wall? Well, actually, it is more than a wall. It is a whole ceiling—in the chapel Pope Sixtus built. It is rather bare now. Let me know if you're interested, will you? It is a lot of work, sure but I am willing to make it worth your effort. And this— *(Points to the fresco)* Great job, excellent, yes indeed! *(Pause)* Come, Çesare—I would like to visit *il Duomo*, before heading back.

Exit the **Pope** *and his entourage, including* **Çesare***.*

Machiavelli *walks up to* **Leonardo***.*

MACHIAVELLI: I told you the Moor was finished. Now, don't think of it as losing a patron, think of it as gaining a Pope. *(Pause)* Where's what's—his name? Salai? *(Pause)* Well, I must be going. You have made some powerful friends, Maestro. I am sure we will see each other again.

Exit **Machiavelli**.

Slow blackout on the refectory as **Leonardo**, *stunned, stares at the wall.*

Scene xv

Downstage, **Stage Left:** *A cell*.

Enter the **Old Man**.

Stage Right: Leonardo's *apartments*.

Enter **Leonardo** *and the boys*.

OLD MAN: It was nearly six o'clock when we got home. It was already dark outside. Maestro Leonardo went straight up to his room. We sat around and wondered. Although he had not said anything we knew there was a good possibility that we might all have to return to our families, especially if Maestro Leonardo did not find a new engagement soon.

The **Old Man** *takes a quick look at his book.*

OLD MAN: *(Pause)* Oh, I almost forgot; we were getting ready for bed, when—

SOUND: Loud knocks on the door.

OLD MAN: Knocks on the door at night made people nervous because most of the time it was soldiers waiting to take you away.
LEONARDO: *(Off)* Will someone see who's there!
MARCO: Don't look at me. I'm tired.
ANTONIO: You lazy bastard!
LORENZO: And I am going to bed.

Exit **Lorenzo** *and* **Marco**.

SOUND: Loud knocks on the door.

LEONARDO: *(Off)* Open the door—or else!
OLD MAN: I thought it was Sofia—
ANTONIO: Sofia, is it you?

With the **Old Man** *narrating,* **Antonio** *grabs a dagger from the table, a torch from the wall and goes to open the door.*

OLD MAN: Except that Sofia was by then fast asleep in her room which was all the way in the back of the house so, even if she had been awake, she would never have heard someone knocking at the door. In other words, it was up to me to risk my life!

ANTONIO: Who's there?

OLD MAN: It took me a second to recognize the apparition staring at me.

Antonio *screams.*

OLD MAN: The ghost was filthy with a bloated, bloody face. The ghost had patches of very short hair on its head and the ghost was in rags.

ANTONIO: *(Trembling)* Who are you? What do you want?

Enter **Salai**.

ANTONIO: *(Screams)* Oh, God! Don't hurt me! I always treated you nice! Don't hurt me, I beg you! I was your friend! What are you doing coming back from the dead!

SALAI: *(Laughs)* Oh, you whoreson! Don't make me laugh—oh, that hurts!

ANTONIO: SALAI!!!

OLD MAN: It was a very alive, if smelly Salai!

ANTONIO: Salai! Salai! He's alive! Salai is alive!

Antonio *runs up and down, calling everyone in the house. First* **Lorenzo** *and* **Marco**, *then* **Sofia** *and finally,* **Leonardo** *rush in the room. They greet the boy between tears of joy, laughter, hugs and kisses.*

LEONARDO: Oh, my sweet, sweet boy!

OLD MAN: *(Pause)* There were more questions than answers but Maestro Leonardo decided they would wait; Salai was having trouble talking and walking. We helped him to his room and even gave him a bath! After thinking about it—why Salai was not put to death, as ordered by the Moor, Maestro Leonardo guessed that his

OLD MAN: *(Cont.)* –offer to the executioners had not been in vain. They had thought of a way to switch Salai with another prisoner in the dungeon, so they could later exchange the young apprentice for the gold Maestro Leonardo promised them. That was the reason they cut Salai's hair, so they could glue it on the other man. After a switch of clothes, the other fellow—who was dead by then—was hung from the tower. The plan would have worked if Bernardino da Corte had not betrayed the Moor. *(Pause)* When news of his daughter's murder reached the Duke of Ferrara, he placed an enormous bounty on Bernardino; the counselor was tracked down, tortured, disemboweled and cut to pieces; his remains scattered on the streets to feed rats and stray dogs. *(Pause)* Ludovico Sforza, the Moor of Milan never recovered from the betrayal. "Since Judas," he liked to say, "there was never such treason!" He died in a French prison cell at the age of fifty-four. *(Pause)* Shortly after unveiling the fresco, Lorenzo decided that it was time to set out on his own. It was not an easy decision because we were all very good friends— and fond of Maestro Leonardo. *(Pause)* Marco too, left soon after that. Since he could not earn a living as an artist, he became a carpenter, took a wife and died of old age. According to his eldest son, Marco spent the last year of his life muttering the names of Leonardo da Vinci and a beautiful wench called Salai. *(Pause)* You already know what happened to me so I will not dwell on it further except to say that I was the only fool to ever try Leonardo Da Vinci's spectacular flying machine. It happened one day, during an outing to the country, when Salai was still recuperating from his wounds. *(Pause)* Because he was too weak and Lorenzo was too big and Marco was too heavy, I volunteered to get strapped to the leather wings, then was pushed off a cliff by Maestro Leonardo. He was very confident that I would soar like a— *(Pause-sighs)* Well, let's just say I did not fly and have been limping ever since. *(Pause)* Maestro Leonardo and Salai left Milan in 1499 and for a time, settled in Rome, where the artist turned military engineer, working for none other than Çesare Borgia. Not long after that, Maestro Leonardo found himself another young apprentice, a noble youth of seventeen, named Francesco Melzi. *(Pause)* Maestro Leonardo was sixty years old. *(Pause)* Salai was thirty-one and he, at last, had run out of patience with his master—jealousy probably had a

OLD MAN: *(Cont.)* –lot to do with it. He not only moved out but took with him most of Maestro Leonardo's paintings, including a portrait of a woman fondly remembered as the <u>Mona Lisa</u>. *(Pause)* Around this time, Leonardo Da Vinci and his new apprentice went to live in France where Maestro Leonardo died in 1519; only Melzi was at his bedside. Yet, in his last will and testament, the great Leonardo bequeathed "his servant Salai" a plot of land outside Milan; one given to the artist by his patron Ludovico the Moor "in lieu of payment for services rendered." *(Pause)* Gian Giacomo Caproti, known to his master, lover and teacher as Salai died in 1524 of a gunshot wound during a quarrel.

As the **Old Man** *narrates* **Downstage,** *the* **Lights** *come up on the refectory .*

OLD MAN: *(Pause)* Today Leonardo da Vinci's *Cenacolo* is an indistinguishable blob. Then again, its condition, which barely hints to the original, gives it a mystical aura that has compelled generations to think of it as something it never was. I am sure that Maestro Leonardo would have been quite pleased and surprised that he had finally achieved the fame he so desperately sought in life. *(Pause)* Most extraordinary of all, I think, was his revenge.

The **Old Man** *slowly goes to black, as a* **Spot** *narrows its scope, spotlighting only the face of Judas, on the fresco.*

OLD MAN: *(Off)* Only days after unveiling *the Cenacolo*, the good brothers at the monastery noticed that something was happening to the fresco on their wall; it seemed that the horrible, evil looking profile representing the Judas began to fade and, as if by magic, another face appeared underneath. According to those who witnessed the transformation, the Judas bore a striking resemblance to the once ruling Duke of Milan.

Lights *go to black.*

End Of The Play

Prop List & Sound SFX

Candle stub (1)
Wooden box (1)
Manuscript (1)
Quill (1)
Bags of candy (2)
Fancy box of candy (2)
A note (2)
Sign: "Tomassino-Sweets" (2)
Work benches (5)
Large tarp (5)
Large scaffold (5)
Tool boxes (5)
Work tables (5)
Brushes (5)
Bowls of pigment (5)
Il Cenacolo (6)
Bernardino's table (9)
Small statue of a horse (13)
Wine glasses (27)
Several drawings (27)
Dishes (27)
Silverware (27)
Notebook and pencils (29)
Bowl of pigment (36)
A map (44)
Coins (48)
Knife (48)
Green vial (48)
Purse (48)
Lute (55)
Bucket (59)
Brush dripping red paint (62)
Blanket (67)
Costumes for Beatrice (71)
Candlestick (73)
Divan (74)
Bowl of plaster (77)

Bags of pigment (77)
A drawing (77)
Apron (78)
Pieces of candy (79)
Knives (82)
Branding irons (82)
Spikes (82)
Axes (82)
Vises (82)
Hooks (82)
Saws (82)
Ropes (5, 82)
Torture rack (82)
Ludovico's bee costume (88)
Statuette of the horse (89)
A leather strap (90)
Huge blade (91)
Carving knife (93)
Notebook and pencil (93)
Thief's knife (93)
A letter (96)
Pope's table (96)
Notebook (99)
Wet plaster (99)
The scaffold (61, 101)
Box of candy (73, 79, 103)
Candy (9, 103)
Dressing table (103)
Ornate chair (104)
Gold rope (104)
Red carpet (104)
Embroidered cover (104)
Old man's book (108)
A torch (109)
A dagger (109)
The finished Cenacolo (111)

Sound SFX

The choir of friars in the background (5)
Friars singing in the background (36)
Patrons talking and laughing and other noise (48)
Rain and thunder (64, 66)
Cries of "murder" and "stop! Murderer!" (74)
Banging on the door (74)
A choir of friars sing (77)
Sofia screams (92)
Trumpet call (102)
Trumpets call (103)
Loud knocks on the door (108)